WILD CALIFORNIA

Peregrine Falcons, North Coast Range, California

WILD CALIFORNIA

Vanishing Lands, Vanishing Wildlife

A. Starker Leopold

Text

Tupper Ansel Blake

Photographs

Contributions by Raymond F. Dasmann

UNIVERSITY OF CALIFORNIA PRESS

Published in cooperation with
THE NATURE CONSERVANCY

The publication of this book was made possible
in part by the generous assistance of The Nature
Conservancy.

University of California Press
Berkeley and Los Angeles, California
University of California Press, Ltd.
London, England

Printed in Japan

2   3   4   5   6   7   8   9

Library of Congress Cataloging in Publication Data

Leopold, A. Starker (Aldo Starker), 1913
Wild California.

Bibliography: p.
1. Ecology—California.   2. Nature conservation—
California.   I. Blake, Tupper Ansel.   II. Dasmann,
Raymond Fredric, 1919–   .   III. Title.
QH105.C2L46   1985   574.9794   85-1131
ISBN 0-520-05293-5

To all those who help conserve, protect, and restore
California's wild lands and wildlife,
"things natural, wild, and free"

CONTENTS

Wild California is a chronicle of California's wild lands and vanishing species. It is a salute to a young photographer, Tupper Ansel Blake, and to a man for all seasons, A. Starker Leopold.

In his gentle and kindly manner, Starker championed the cause of preserving both wild lands and species in his adopted state of California. He anticipated that the magical sounds of the marsh, the booming of the sage grouse, and the mystical roll of the rainbow trout might very well vanish from California. He put his soul and his heart into teaching students, sportsmen, business leaders, and politicians that we have a responsibility to preserve the magic of the marsh and the silence of the forest for our children and theirs.

Twice I visited The Nature Conservancy's McCloud River Preserve with Starker. We stalked the banks for rainbow trout, watching otter and mergansers. My memory of one day is especially vivid: myself in a wild rapid, hooked to a two-pounder, and Starker, hobbled on the bank by a bad back, rooting for both of us simultaneously. His affection encompassed both trout and angler, prey and predator.

An hour or so later, sipping bourbon by the fire, Starker explained to me why he had rooted for the trout. His discourse encompassed aesthetics, education, science, and medicine, in the afterglow of a strong sour mash. His argument (see "The Legacy") subsequently became the inspiration for The Nature Conservancy's effort to protect all of California's threatened species and ecosystems.

Starker's impact extended beyond the river. At the California Nature Conservancy's first board meeting, he inspired his fellow directors to undertake the California Critical Areas Program, a $15 million thrust to preserve California's threatened natural heritage. His comments ranged from natural history anecdotes to philosophy, and his warmth and wisdom inspired this assembly of business leaders and conservationists. Two weeks later, on an excursion to Santa Cruz Island, I overheard one Nature Conservancy director, the chairman of a leading bank, using Starker's lessons to convert a corporate executive into a conservation supporter.

Tupper, Starker, and I began *Wild California* one year before Starker's death. I was a latecomer to the project, but grateful that The Nature Conservancy would be participating.

Starker Leopold passed away in the middle of the project. His friend and student, Raymond Dasmann, has sewn the pieces together beautifully, and I am certain that Starker would be happy that so many of us are continuing his work.

Peter Seligmann
January 1985

PREFACE

Shortly before Starker Leopold's death in August 1983, I visited with him in his office in Mulford Hall at the University of California, Berkeley. Not surprisingly, we talked about books. He had great enthusiasm for the writing he was doing and spoke with appreciation of the photographs Tupper Blake had taken to illustrate their planned volume on wild California.

When Peter Seligmann called me to ask if I would be willing to undertake the completion of Starker's writings, I could only say yes. My debt to Starker and my appreciation of all he had done was enough to give this task a high priority. Unfortunately, I did not know what was involved. I had visions of piles of manuscripts left in some half-finished stage and of stacks of old unpublished speeches. There was no such material. Starker had finished five chapters. For the rest I had to seek out already published writings. As time permitted, I reread virtually everything Starker published. Much of it is of a technical nature not suited to this volume. But here and there are descriptive, philosophical, or advocative pieces that I believed could be put together to illuminate collectively Starker's principal interests and concerns.

This is obviously not the book Starker would have written. I hope, however, that it helps to recapture some of his personality, sense of humor, and personal concern. It will be apparent to the reader that Starker never ceased to be involved with the future of wildlife and of wild California.

Raymond F. Dasmann
June 1984

ACKNOWLEDGMENTS

In the fall of 1979 a historic and unprecedented photographic survey of the wildlife and wild lands of California was launched under the sponsorship of the National Audubon Society and the California Department of Fish and Game. Its purpose was to record the richness and diversity of wild California and document the status of our wildlife and its habitats as the twentieth century drew to a close.

In the task of carrying out the photographic fieldwork I received help from many people and, in particular, the guidance and encouragement of A. Starker Leopold. Special mention should be made of the support given by Paul Howard and Richard Martyr of the National Audubon Society and by Jim Messersmith and John Mackenzie of the California Department of Fish and Game. I would also like to thank Sherman Chickering, The David and Lucille Packard Foundation, The Dean Witter Foundation, The Atholl McBean Foundation, and the California Academy of Sciences for their early support of and continuing enthusiasm for this California wildlife project.

For making it possible to turn the original photographic survey into the images in this book, I make grateful acknowledgment of the help of Peter Seligmann, director, California Nature Conservancy; James H. Clark, director, University of California Press; Ray Dasmann, professor of environmental studies, University of California, Santa Cruz, who upon Starker Leopold's death graciously agreed to complete the text; and Elizabeth Leopold, Starker's wife, who encouraged us to go on with the book. A very special acknowledgment is made to The Nature Conservancy, whose generous support made this project possible.

Last, but by no means least, I am indebted to my wife, Sandraline Cedarwall Blake, who coordinated the entire photographic project from fund raising to fieldwork to museum exhibition. She shared my camps from the sage-scented Great Basin to the salt-sprayed offshore islands; from the stillness of the desert to the bug-buzzing wetlands of the Central Valley. Her counsel and untiring efforts made possible the completion of the survey and allowed this photographer to practice his craft. There is a bit of Sandy in each image presented here.

Tupper Ansel Blake
October 1984

WILD CALIFORNIA

Oak Woodland, Central Coast Range, California

1 :: THE LEGACY

Of the sixty-eight oak tree species that grow in the United States, fifteen are found in California. The California live oak grows on the lower slopes and in the valleys of the central Coast Range. It is an evergreen with a broad, low crown and hollylike leaves. Called encina *by early Spanish and Mexican settlers, California live oaks thrive amid our grasslands and provide excellent habitat for wildlife, furnishing food for the acorn woodpecker and the black-tailed deer in one instance and serving as a nesting platform for a pair of golden eagles in another.*

Spanish settlement of California began in 1769 with the establishment of a mission at San Diego. In the next twenty years the good friars extended the influence of the church up the coast to San Francisco. Their written chronicles tell us more about the aborigines whose souls needed saving than about the countryside in which those souls resided. But what a countryside it must have been! Oak woodland in the valley and foothills, extensive meadows of wildflowers, running streams in the canyons, and estuaries rich with shore life along the coast. Only in the higher coastal mountains did the chaparral form something of a barrier to easy travel.

European seafarers who followed the friars—Jean François de Galaup de la Pérouse in 1786, Archibald Menzies and Captain George Vancouver in 1790, and others—left for our edification vivid descriptions of the charm of coastal California, then only slightly changed by Spanish settlement. Beaver trappers and mountain men who came later—John Work of the Hudson's Bay Company, Jedediah Smith, Zenas Leonard, George Nidiver—added fascinating details of the landscapes in the mountains of northern and eastern California and in the great Central Valley. As outdoorsmen living on the country, these men spoke knowingly and with great appreciation of the abundance of elk, bears, beavers, and waterfowl in the Central Valley and of the deer in the adjoining foothills. Others described with wonder the stately forests of sequoia and fir along the north coast and the tremendous runs of salmon that seasonally ascended the coastal rivers. Anyone who enjoys reading these historical descriptions of original California cannot help but be awed by the richness and variety of the landscape as we inherited it.

All of that changed rapidly, of course. Even before the discovery of gold, a continuous stream of settlers poured west, seeking to homestead the most fertile and productive parts of California—the valleys, the north coast forests, and the oases in the desert. Eventually, the exploitable resources were reduced to possession, until the landscape today would scarcely be recognizable to those who saw it in its pristine form. Valley lands are almost entirely converted to agriculture. Most of the fresh water has been dammed, diverted, and ditched to produce power or irrigate crops. Forests have been cut and recut and now in great areas are being replaced with even-aged conifer plantations. Tremendous areas of formerly productive land have been converted to cities or paved over as highways, airports, or supermarket parking lots. Nor is the rate of change decreasing; it is, in fact, still accelerating as the human population continues to rise.

Fortunately, there are still recognizable patches of the old California left. Some of the original ecosystems are well represented in parks, national forests, and public domain lands. Mountain tops and some forest types are generously preserved. Big blocks of desert are held in reserved status, although much of the desert is being battered by motorcycles and vacationers. But other important landscapes have been reduced to tattered remnants. Riparian woodlands, for example, which played so important a role in supporting wildlife and the aboriginal peoples in the Central Valley, are nearly gone. So also are the perennial grasslands, the vernal pools, the interior tule marshes, and the valley woodlands. If samples of old California are to be saved, they will have to be identified and set aside quickly lest they disappear while we are preparing to act.

There are several good reasons for preserving adequate samples of *all* ecosystems, and not just those that are scenic or spectacular. The first and most obvious justification of natural area preservation is the aesthetic and educational value—we should know and be able to show future generations the landscapes from which modern California was carved. But of equal significance is the scientific, "baseline" value of retaining combinations of soils, plants, and animals that formed the fertile ground we now exploit with such abandon. When irrigation water is carried to desert soils, the land bursts with productivity. If yields lag, we pour on fertilizers. Will the land stand up indefinitely under such pressure? Might there be colloidal changes in the soil that are irreversible? Is there a chance that some day we might want to reexamine the original soil type to see what changes we have created? In this sense, samples of arable land may prove to be the most important of natural areas. Similarly, native forest types of mixed conifers and hardwoods may retain fertility better than pure conifer plantations. Livestock ranges of shrubs and native grasses may in the end outproduce pure stands of crested wheatgrass. Finally, fully 50 percent of all pharmaceuticals have a natural component as the active ingredient; yet only 2 percent of the world's plants have been analyzed and tested. Countless potential benefits for mankind certainly lie locked within many of these untested species. Simply stated, society depends on the complete array of plants and animals found in whole, undisturbed ecosystems for food, medicine, clothing, and shelter.

There is growing recognition that natural areas should be preserved, although the diverse reasons may not always be understood. But who is responsible for the total preservation program? Various government agencies contribute in a number of ways, but some ecosystems, such as riparian woodlands, do not fit neatly into any government program. There remains an important role for private initiative, both in the purchase or leasing of lands for conservation purposes and in the management of privately owned lands to provide for long-term conservation values. The Nature Conservancy has played a leading role both in identifying areas that should be better protected and in taking the initiative to provide that protection. The importance of its effort cannot be overstated.

A. Starker Leopold
November 1981

Mill Creek, Mount Lassen, California

Waterfalls, streams, and lakes; ice, snow, and glaciers—water in its many and varied forms adds immeasurably to the aesthetic and recreational appeal of the Sierra Nevada and the Cascades. Water is the chief erosive force that gradually modifies the landscape. The action of water on the land is varied, from the slight expansion of seepage freezing in a rock crevice to the colossal force of a slow-moving glacier to the powerful transport of a fast stream such as Mill Creek flowing down from the western slope of Mount Lassen during the summer snow melt.

Soda Lake, Carrizo Plain, California

4

A winter sunrise, bringing warmth and color to the grasslands of the Carrizo Plain, marks the beginning of a new day for Soda Lake and the Temblor Range beyond. Soda Lake and its surrounding habitat form an alkaline salt marsh ecosystem of pristine quality. Due to its location be- *tween the Central Valley and the coast, an unusual mix of plants occurs. Given their isolation, Soda Lake and the Carrizo Plain offer habitat for large numbers of wintering wading birds, raptors, shore-birds, and waterfowl.*

Kern Canyon, Greenhorn Mountains, California

The San Joaquin Valley is almost completely enclosed by mountains, the basin's only outlet being the San Joaquin–Sacramento River delta in the north. To the south, the valley is bordered by the Tehachapi Mountains and, in the east, by the Sierra Nevada. Springtime brings myriad wildflowers to carpet these eastern foothills, which are quite steep and rugged where the rivers and streams of the high Sierra rush to the valley floor.

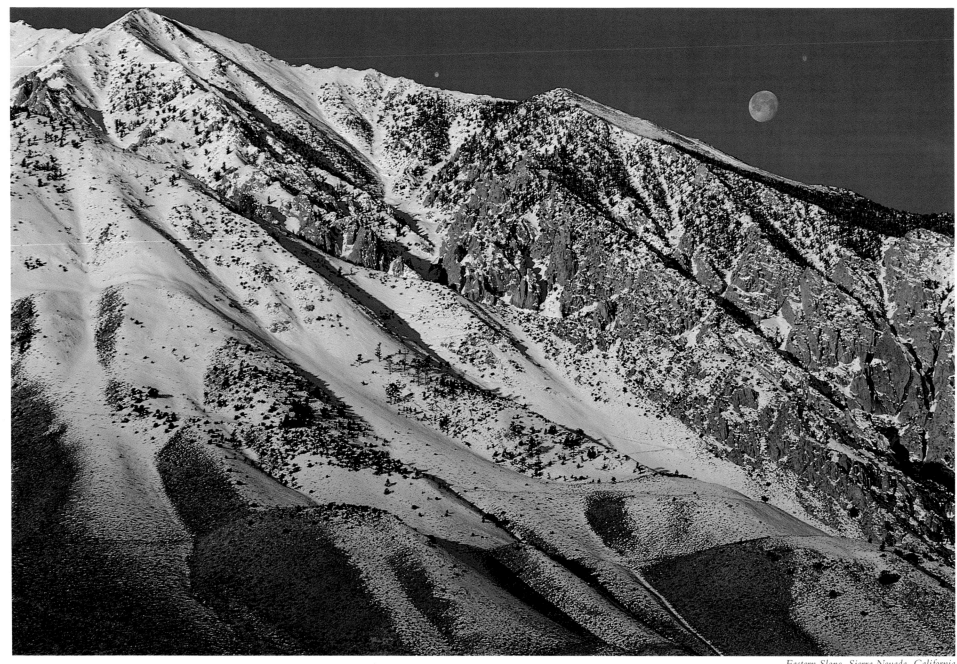

Eastern Slope, Sierra Nevada, California

Called una gran sierra nevada—*a great snow-covered mountain range—by the early Spanish, and later labeled the "cathedral of light" by John Muir, the Sierra Nevada continues to awe all who view it. This mountain range forms the major part of California's eastern border, running some four hundred miles and separating the Great Basin from the great Central Valley. To this day, the Sierra Nevada's diverse range of habitats, from foothills to conifer forests to the high country, provides an equally diverse flora and fauna.*

Drake's Bay, Point Reyes, California

Plant and animal communities, even those of the salt marsh, are dependent on the open water of the bays along the coastline. At low tide, broad mudflats yield rich marine life vital to the existence of hundreds of thousands of shorebirds. As the tide rises along the bay's rich fringe, it carries food and oxygen across the mudflats and into the salt marsh. Receding again, it flushes away wastes in the elegant, rhythmic tidal cycle that is essential to all life of the bay.

California Sea Lions, San Miguel Island, California

8

With six species of pinnipeds inhabiting its shores, San Miguel Island can justifiably be called one of the world's most diversified rookeries of marine mammals. On this isolated Channel Island are northern fur seals, Steller sea lions, northern elephant seals, California sea lions, harbor seals, and Guadalupe fur seals.

Snow Geese and Cackling Geese, Tule Lake, Klamath Basin, California

The Klamath Basin hosts one of the largest concentrations of migratory waterfowl to be found in the world. Though the large, shallow lakes and extensive marshes of this region occupy only one-fifth of their former acreage, they retain their importance to the wildlife they sustain. Each year, the majority of the waterfowl of the Pacific flyway (peak numbers of up to one million birds in one day) funnel through the basin during their migration.

9

Joshua Trees, Castle Peaks Wilderness, Mojave Desert, California

The desert often seems monotonous, gray, and vast. In the dry season (which is most of the time), the traveler views mile upon mile of neatly spaced creosote bushes, with an occasional cluster of cactus or a stringer of desert willow along a dry wash. In the heat of midday, animal life is conspicuously absent. Coming suddenly upon a desert spring, then, is like finding an island in the ocean. The concentration of life is startling—the vegetation is a healthy green rather than gray, and there is a scurrying and fluttering of birds and small mammals.

Under a spreading mesquite, whose branches form an umbrella, a covey of Gambel quail may be found loafing. Their soft chirping is an expression of mutual reassurance that all is well. In the season of drought, the quail come daily to drink, and once there, they often linger through the day. Morning and evening the quail forage over the desert for distances up to half a mile, scratching in the sand for the seeds of weeds and wildflowers that fruited and died with the last rains. After the late feeding the birds return to the spring to seek safe roosts in the trees or tall shrubs, above reach of the prowling bobcat and under a leafy canopy that hides them from the hunting owl. The numbers of Gambel quail frequenting a spring may vary from a mere handful in dry years to hundreds in years of generous rainfall.

Wildflowers carpet the desert in wet years, and the quail browse on the tender leaves of the growing plants, which seem to contain some nutritive element that stimulates the urge to mate and nest. The males fight raucously over mates, and even after all the females are claimed, the excess males call persistently. In such a year of sexual enthusiasm, many young are reared, and, fortunately, the robust stands of annual plants scatter their seeds abundantly, so that there is adequate food to support the expanded quail population through the year.

The Joshua tree, as the dominant species in its habitat, is a foundation of life for surrounding animal communities. Its blossoms feed yucca moths, and its fallen branches or litter host nocturnal desert lizards. Twenty-five species of desert birds nest in the Joshua tree, and small mammals use its leaves for constructing their nests.

Quite the opposite situation applies in a dry year. Wildflowers are stunted, and although the quail eat the fresh leaves, there are chemicals (steroids) that seem to suppress the mating urge rather than stimulate it. Under the worst conditions the quail do not even pair off and nest, but remain in winter coveys and conserve their strength for another year. Individuals die in one way or another, and the flocks dwindle until, after several successive years of poor reproduction, a pitiful remnant of old birds persists. When at last another lush year comes, a big crop of young is raised, and quail are abundant once again. Boom and bust is the rule on the desert, and quail, along with other life forms, reflect these oscillations. In bust years the desert spring is a crucial key to the continuity of many species, quail included. Without the spring, the remnants would never make it through protracted years of drought.

The welfare of desert rodents is similarly affected by the vagaries of weather. Abundant seeds that nurture quail after a good growing year are also the staff of life for ground squirrels, kangaroo rats, pocket mice, and other small mammals. Most desert rodents gather seeds when they are easily available and store them in underground caches for periods of scarcity. Such food storage is a form of insurance not available to quail. Another advantage is the ability of rodents to hibernate in burrows when conditions on the surface are unfavorable. In protracted periods of either drought or cold, rodents can curl up and sleep until things get better. The deep sleep of hibernation is accompanied by a drop in body temperature, sometimes approaching the ambient temperature of the burrow. In this manner the little mammal conserves food—both that stored in the body as fat and the seeds stored in the burrow. But all these ploys for survival of the individual do not of themselves stimulate the animals to reproduce. Just as in the case of the quail, nutritive elements produced in green leaves following adequate rain apparently stimulate sexual enthusiasm in desert rodents. Big litters of healthy young are the consequence. Jackrabbits respond in much the same way, and occasionally when some desert locality has been favored with good rains several years in a row, the jackrabbit population may increase to the point where highways become littered with bodies struck down by automobiles at night.

Boom years for the small vertebrates become, in turn, boom years for the desert predators. Hawks, owls, foxes, coyotes, and bobcats all respond to abundance of prey by successfully rearing more young of their own. Studies in a desert valley in Utah have shown a positive correlation between the population of jackrabbits and the number of coyote pups raised. Jackrabbits constituted well over half the diet of the breeding coyotes, small rodents being of less importance. Persistent coyote predation on jackrabbits was shown to reduce their numbers considerably in years of poor rabbit reproduction, and then coyote reproduction in turn would fall off. But in a boom year, jackrabbits raising four or five litters per season jumped numerically far ahead of their enemies, and it then became the turn of the coyote to catch up. This teeter-totter relationship between these two cohabitants of the desert has presumably continued for eons.

Larger animals associated with the desert waterhole are buffeted less by ephemeral changes in weather. Bighorn sheep and mule deer are long-lived compared to rabbits, rodents, and coyotes, and they have evolved techniques for outlasting periods of adversity. The waterhole is essential to their existence in hot, dry spells, but unlike quail or coyotes, they do not have to drink every day. Even in hot summer weather, bighorns have been known to get along without drinking for periods of up to a week, which permits them to forage far from the waterhole. In such circumstances the animals return to the drinking place badly desiccated and may take on water up to 20 percent of body weight. Desert mule deer likewise can go for at least a couple of days without drinking. But water deprivation is not the normal choice of these animals. They prefer to drink daily if circumstances permit. Daily drinking, however, means that foraging must take place within a limited radius of the water source. When nearby food is exhausted, the foraging circle must be extended. If domestic animals such as sheep, cattle, or burros have access to the same spring, the depletion of food is greatly accelerated, to the decided disadvantage of the deer and the bighorns.

A. Starker Leopold
November 1981

Coyotes, Santa Rosa Mountains, California

The coyote of the desert is paler and smaller than its cousins, the coastal and mountain coyotes. This is due to its meager diet, to high summer temperatures, and to occasional long periods of severe drought when most of the small rodents and insects on which it feeds perish. What this beneficial predator lacks in size, it certainly makes up for in sound. To those who have heard the coyote around their camp at dusk or have been awakened at dawn and heard its song to the sun, a desert without the coyote would be barren indeed.

13

Antelope Ground Squirrel and Gambel Quail, Santa Rosa Mountains, California

14

"Food chain" is a process by which food energy is exchanged between organisms interrelated by their feeding habits, smaller ones being fed upon by larger ones that, in turn, feed still larger ones. The antelope ground squirrel and Gambel quail survive by eating plant material. These animals may then provide a meal for a coyote.

West of Kelso Dunes, Mojave Desert, California

The wide vistas of rugged desert wilderness
encompass myriad wonders that demand
the admiration and surprise of the beholder.
California's rich desert heritage is one of
unequaled natural beauty. The wildlife
and wildlands of the desert are treasures
and resources to be cherished and protected
for all time.

Red Diamond Rattlesnake, Morongo Pass, California

Reptiles are the most conspicuous animals of the desert. Each of the various lizards and snakes has adapted to a particular way of defending itself. Rattlesnakes employ their well-known defense of discharging poison through their fangs when they bite. The poisonous red diamond rattlesnake should certainly be avoided but never destroyed, for it plays a vital role in maintaining the delicate balance of the desert ecosystem.

Roadrunner, Furnace Creek, Death Valley, California

Finding a location in the desert to its liking, the roadrunner stays put and makes no regular migration. Preying on lizards, horned toads, grasshoppers, and other insects, as well as on snakes and baby rabbits, this bird of the cuckoo family prefers the protection of dense, thorn-covered mesquite. It depends on its legs for movement, using its wings only as a last resort.

Cooper's Hawk, Morongo Valley, California

A riparian forest is one that grows along watercourses. In the dry desert these forests appear as a green belt. These bright green ribbons of willows, cottonwoods, and other plants provide food and shelter for wildlife. Breeding bird densities in these cottonwood-willow forests equal or exceed those in any California vegetative type. In the cover of the forest canopy flourish insects that are eaten by foraging warblers. These small birds in turn become prey for the Cooper's hawk.

Harris' Hawk, Lower Colorado River, California

The beautiful Harris' hawk has been successfully reintroduced to the valley of the lower Colorado River in the California desert. This raptor hunts a variety of desert prey: reptiles such as lizards, birds such as green-winged teal, and mammals such as cottontail rabbits. In action and flight, the Harris' hawk combines beauty and grace.

19

California Fan Palms, Hidden Palms Oasis, Santa Rosa Mountains, California

Few and far between, desert oases are the true treasures of this arid land. Here, water seeps to the surface giving life to plant and animal alike. Mud or damp sand around the oasis provides a Who's Who of desert dwellers in the form of tracks left behind, for many animals come to the oasis for water, plant food, and prey. Here, too, grows the California fan palm, the only palm tree native to California. The leaves of the palm provide shelter and nest sites for the hooded oriole, and the nuts and berries are eaten by the coyote.

Peninsular Bighorn Sheep, Santa Rosa Mountains, California

Amid the harsh, rocky ranges jutting up
from California's low desert plains live
two subspecies, or races, of desert bighorn
sheep. The Nelson and the peninsular
bighorn require certain basic factors in their
habitat to ensure their survival: food, water, open space, and escape terrain.

Lower Klamath Lake, Klamath Basin, California

3 :: THE GREAT BASIN

Between the Warner Mountains in north-eastern California and the Cascade Range far to the west is a high, semi-arid plateau that is part of a great volcanic field. With an average elevation of 4,500 feet above sea level, the Modoc Plateau region features snow, ice, and frozen lakes as part of its yearly cycle. As the plateau was being formed by the eruptions of the Modoc lavas, it was broken by numerous faults. The results of movements along the faults are conspicuously expressed in the landscape. The northern part of the region, especially near the basins of Lower Klamath, Tule, and Clear lakes, shows a series of fault scarps that are, for the most part, oriented toward the north.

Colonel John C. Frémont defined and named the Great Basin as follows: The Sierra Nevada, he wrote, "forms the western limit of the fertile and timbered lands along the desert and mountainous region included within the Great Basin—a term which I apply to the intermediate region between the Rocky Mountains and the next range (Sierra Nevada), containing many lakes, with their own system of rivers and creeks (of which the Great Salt is the principal) and which have no connection with the ocean." There are many mountain ranges in the Great Basin, most of them minor in size, all of them oriented north and south. Between the ranges are extensive arid valleys where the sage and the jackrabbit predominate.

Sagebrush (*Artemisia tridentata*) is an aromatic shrub capable of growing in arduous habitats. Where soil moisture is reasonably good, the plant reaches seven or eight feet in height in dense stands. On dry hillsides height may be measured in inches, and plants are widely spaced. Though not considered prime forage for either livestock or wildlife, the leaves and twigs are eaten by many ungulate mammals and by at least one bird, the sagehen. Originally, much of the Great Basin was covered with a mixture of perennial grasses and scattered shrubs, primarily sage. Persistent heavy grazing by livestock tended to thin or eliminate the perennial grasses and highly edible forbs and shrubs, permitting the proliferation of sagebrush and various other shrubs of marginal palatability and annual grasses such as cheatgrass. In this continuing process, much of the land's carrying capacity for wildlife has been lost.

The pronghorn antelope was once abundant and widely distributed on the plains of the Great Basin, but remnant populations today are local in distribution and modest in number. In California, a few thousand antelope still exist in Modoc and Lassen counties. Efforts to re-establish them in Mono County have had limited success to date. Broad-leaved forbs are prime forage for pronghorns, and they are scarce on livestock ranges nowadays. Livestock competition likewise may explain why bighorn sheep have not reoccupied their former haunts in the arid ranges of the Great Basin. Livestock not only compete for forage but they have also served to introduce exotic diseases to which bighorns are particularly susceptible. A recent attempt to re-introduce bighorns in Lava Beds National Monument was frustrated by an outbreak of disease that completely destroyed the population when it seemed well on its way to establishment. The disease presumably was brought into the area by domestic sheep.

As noted by Frémont, the rivers of the Great Basin all flow into inland lakes or "seas," where the water evaporates, leaving accumulated salts. Some of these lakes, such as Pyramid Lake in Nevada, are not too salty for fish life. The Truckee River flows east off the Sierra Nevada, through Lake Tahoe and down the Truckee Canyon to Pyramid, where originally there was a fantastic fishery of cutthroat trout. In January of 1844 Frémont camped at the mouth of the Truckee, where he recorded the following: "An Indian brought in a large fish to trade, which we had the inexpressible satisfaction to find was a salmon-trout; we gathered round him eagerly. The Indians were amazed with our delight, and immediately brought in numbers, so that the camp was soon stocked. Their flavor was excellent—superior, in fact, to that of any fish I have ever known. They were of extraordinary size . . . generally from two to four feet in length." This great resource nourished many a traveler during the early years of California's exploration, but spawning runs up the Truckee River were interrupted by dams and diversions, and the cutthroats were replaced in the river by exotic rainbow and brown trout, so that only remnant populations of the native fish remain today.

Mono Lake some miles to the south receives the flow of the Leevining River, or at least did so until the water was diverted into flumes headed for Los Angeles. The lake has always been far more saline than Pyramid, and it supports brine flies rather than fish. William Brewer visited the lake in 1863 and noted: "No fish or reptile lives in it, yet it

Rimrock and lava bed bighorn are other frequently used names for the California bighorn sheep, one of the ten subspecies of sheep native to North America. Those names are appropriate for this race of wild sheep, for they describe the habitat of the bighorn in the Great Basin of California. Mature rams group themselves in bands called "bachelor groups," which do not associate with ewes, yearlings, or lambs except during the breeding season. California bighorn populations are low at present, but great efforts are now being made to improve and protect bighorn ranges, as well as to reintroduce herds into ancestral locations.

California Bighorn Sheep, Klamath Basin, California

swarms with millions of worms, which develop into flies. . . . The number and quantity of these worms and flies is absolutely incredible. They drift up in heaps along the shore—*hundreds of bushels* could be collected. . . . The Indians come from far and near to gather them. The worms are dried in the sun, the shell rubbed off, when a yellowish kernel remains, like a small yellow grain of rice. This is oily, very nutritious, and not unpleasant to the taste. . . . Gulls, ducks, snipe, frogs, and Indians fatten on it."

During the summer the island in Mono Lake has traditionally been a primary nesting ground for the California gull. Thousands of pairs nested there, and their eggs were objects of commerce during the gold-mining era. In autumn, the lake with its bounty of brine flies is a traditional gathering area for migrating grebes and phalaropes. With the present diversion of water away from the lake, the level has dropped drastically, salinity is increasing to a point that may exceed the tolerance of the brine flies, and the value of Mono Lake as a bird habitat may be severely impaired.

Besides inland lakes such as Pyramid and Mono that are a heritage from the great post-glacial Lake Lahontan, there exist in the Great Basin a number of tiny springs and waterholes with their own endemic fish faunas. The most interesting of these fishes are the pupfishes of the genus *Cyprinodon*, which have persisted in microhabitats measured in square feet rather than in acres. Along the southern fringe of the Great Basin, in and near Death Valley National Monument, populations of these strange little fishes occur in a number of isolated springs, distributed from Tecopa Hot Springs in the Mojave Desert to Fish Slough in Owens Valley. Of enormous scientific interest, the pupfishes have attracted the attention of conservation organizations and government agencies.

The sage grouse is one of the birds most characteristic of the Great Basin. Although its range extends north and eastward through the Rocky Mountains, its center has always been the sagebrush flats from eastern California through Nevada, southern Oregon, and Idaho to southern Wyoming. In frontier times the bird was abundant and supplied many a pioneer meal. With settlement, the best (most fertile) habitats were converted to agricultural crops, and livestock grazed the rest, with the inevitable resulting loss in grouse populations. Perhaps the most severe impact of grazing occurred along riparian strips bordering streams and drainage channels. In arid country, the vegetation growing in moist soil along watercourses is of enormous importance in supplying food and cover for wild vertebrates, and these amenities are easily destroyed by assembled herds of cattle, horses, or sheep. Adult sage grouse are able to survive eating the aromatic leaves of the sage, but newly hatched chicks need insects and tender leaves of clover or similar forbs, both of which are most available in lush riparian vegetation now largely disrupted as a result of livestock grazing.

But even in reduced numbers, the big grouse continue to add drama to the land of the sage. In spring, cocks gather on a communal strutting ground called a "lek," there to quarrel over territorial boundaries while they await the arrival of the demure hens. The latter arrive singly, wandering through the lek in a most casual manner and in so doing inciting the cocks to frantic dancing and posturing. In due time each hen accepts a mate and thereafter goes about the business of nesting and rearing a brood with no help from the male. In autumn the hens and young gather into "packs," and the males form small separate groups.

The chukar partridge is an exotic game bird that has become completely acclimated to the Great Basin environment. Originally imported in 1928 from Calcutta, India, the bird was raised on game farms, and liberations were made in virtually all parts of California. Populations became established only in semi-arid regions with rainfall of from five to fifteen inches a year. Most of this range is in the Great Basin east of the Sierra Nevada, with a limited extension into the San Joaquin foothills. Unlike the sage grouse, chukars form pairs in spring and both parents rear the brood. Drinking water is essential for survival of the young, and green leaves are important, too, along with insects that thrive on the greenery. In winter, chukars can thrive on seeds of cheatgrass, Russian thistle, and similar weeds that grow abundantly on grazed rangelands, hence livestock do not prejudice the welfare of this bird as severely as they do the sage grouse.

Sage Grouse, Warner Mountains, California

To make the acquaintance of a sage grouse, the largest native grouse in North America, one must go to the barren plains country of the Great Basin, where the sagebrush grows. To the sage grouse, sagebrush is life itself. This aromatic plant furnishes the bird with food and safe cover. Flocks of male sage grouses assemble in earliest spring to croak, strut, and posture on ancestral grounds called "leks." This display of vanity is often punctuated with frequent fights as the males establish a hierarchy in which one will emerge as the dominant breeder.

One of the curious anomalies of animal distribution on the east slope of the Sierra Nevada was the presence of muskrats and the absence of beavers. The muskrat somehow made its way throughout most of the continent from the Colorado River northward to Alaska. It occurred in Surprise Valley in eastern Modoc County but never succeeded in crossing the low divide to the headwaters of the Pit River, and thence to the Sacramento. The introduction of the muskrat into the Central Valley occurred after settlement. The beaver, however, was abundant in the Central Valley but seemingly did not occur on streams draining east from the Sierra Nevada. In 1844, when Frémont and Kit Carson were floundering about in the Truckee and Carson watersheds trying to find a stream draining west to the Sacramento, Frémont wrote: "With every stream I now expected to see the great Buenaventura; and Carson hurried eagerly to search, on every one we reached, for beaver cuttings, which he always maintained we should find only on waters that ran to the Pacific; and the absence of such signs was to him a sure indication that the water had no outlet from the Great Basin." Presumably there were shortcomings in the habitat (lack of aspen, perhaps) that precluded beaver occupancy. Logging and wildfires subsequently produced aspen aplenty. Beavers were introduced in the 1930s and are now present on most east-flowing streams.

Visitors to the eastern foothills of the Sierra Nevada often ask about the conspicuous white blazes that appear on rock outcrops or talus slopes. These are calcareous deposits derived from the urine of the bushy-tailed woodrat. Male woodrats are highly territorial and defend their private rocky domains from other males, though welcoming the presence of several females. Each summer the females bear two or three small litters of young, which are driven into the world upon approaching adulthood to seek their own homes. Young males in particular wander far afield looking for an unoccupied site with shelter suitable for surviving the winter. In autumn they pluck and cure the green leaves of various trees before storing them deep in the rockpile for later use. Aspen leaves are preferred, but dogwood, alder, coffeeberry, and wild cherry may be gathered. With the harvest in, the master rat and his harem are set for winter.

Most of the bald eagles in the state are found wintering around the lakes and marshes of northeastern California. The Klamath Basin and Tule Lake Basin are favorite gathering places for eagles that have migrated from more northerly breeding grounds. The big birds need stout pine trees for roosting, open grown so that there is room to fly in and out. Often roosts are well back in the hills away from bodies of water. For feeding, however, the eagles gravitate to the marshes and lake shores, where dead fish or waterfowl can be scavenged. The seasonal passage of great flocks of ducks and geese, cranes, and even white pelicans that visit these shores is further highlighted by the stately flight of the eagles.

A. Starker Leopold
May 1983

The porcupine, a large, slow-moving rodent, has no real need to live life any other way, for it is one of the most efficiently protected mammals. Its long, stiff spines, which reach their greatest development on its tail and rump, are merely modified hairs. They are loosely attached, and with a swift slap of its spiny tail, the porcupine can drive away a mountain lion. Though porcupines feed primarily on the bark of trees, wandering individuals can be found in the sagebrush flats of the Great Basin, where they feed on sagebrush bark.

Porcupine, Clear Lake, Klamath Basin, California

White Pelicans, Lower Klamath Lake, California

White pelicans need isolation in order to survive. To set up a nesting colony, these pelicans require undisturbed islands in large lakes or marshes. The Great Basin of California provides the necessary habitat. Nesting on barren ground or tule mats, *the rookery thrives on a diet of fish caught in the vicinity by adult birds, which feed their young by regurgitation.*

Mono Lake, California

The high levels of salinity and alkalinity of Mono Lake allow the growth of great densities of brine shrimp and brine flies, which in turn sustain large populations of breeding and wintering migratory birds. A recent count by ornithologists showed that a quarter of the California gull population nested on Mono Lake's Negit Island; summer and fall populations of eared grebes approached one million individuals.

Great Basin Wild Rye, Clear Lake, Klamath Basin, California

The Great Basin offers endless views of a soft gray-green landscape, dominated by low shrubs. The most common of these is the artemisia, or sagebrush, which provides food for many of the birds and mammals of this broad and arid land. Not so prevalent is an equally important plant, the native grass called Great Basin wild rye, a good forage grass eaten by antelope and mule deer. The wild rye, with its creeping rhizomes and spreading roots, is of additional value as a soil and sand binder.

Bald Eagle, Tule Lake, Klamath Basin, California

During winter months, the Klamath Basin holds the largest concentration of bald eagles in the United States, outside of Alaska. Over five hundred of these majestic birds arrive at the basin each year, attracted by the plentiful waterfowl. The eagles begin to alight on the frozen lake each morning before sunrise, preying on crippled or dead birds and often providing a stunning display of aerial skills. When feeding is over, the eagles move to nearby trees to spend the day preening and perching. As sunset draws near, they leave their perches for numerous roosting sites located many miles away in the dense protective cover of the coniferous forest.

Crustose Lichen, New York Mountain Wilderness, Mojave Desert, California

34

Lichens are small colored plants that grow on the surface of rocks and trees, often producing colorful patterns. Most lichens consist of a fungus body combined with colonies of algae. The combination is an example of mutual benefit called symbiosis. As lichens produce strong acids that decompose rocks, even granite, to obtain minerals, they aid in soil formation.

Prairie Falcon, Klamath Basin, California

The prairie falcon nests on cliffs and, being so restricted in its breeding sites, is not a plentiful bird. The prairie falcon can be found hunting in open, treeless country, where in its pursuit of small mammals such as ground squirrels, marmots, and jackrabbits, it descends like a bullet at a long, low angle. This falcon can be distinguished in flight by the quick hard strokes of its slender, pointed wings.

Klamath Basin, California

The cliffs scattered throughout the Great Basin region of California comprise a very important rocky habitat. Cliff swallows, peregrine falcons, prairie falcons, golden eagles, red-tailed hawks, great horned owls, barn owls, and ravens all nest on cliff faces and ledges and in pot holes. Lo- cations vary; cliffs are found at the summits of high mountains and along the steep sides of stream canyons. An excellent vantage point for locating prey, the cliff also affords the benefit of protective cover during bad weather.

Snow Geese and Cackling Geese, Tule Lake, Klamath Basin, California

For centuries plentiful food and cover have annually brought untold numbers of geese from central Canada and the far north to winter in California. The Klamath Basin, located within the Great Basin, is an important stopover in the migration. Hundreds of thousands of geese such as the lesser snow goose and the cackling goose stop to rest and feed here on their way to the Central Valley and points south.

Sage Thrasher, Honey Lake, California

Eager to defend his territory and to attract a female, the male sage thrasher prefers the highest promontory he can find. In the early morning, he mounts the top of a tall sage to pour out a song equal to the mockingbird's in sweetness.

Eared Grebes, Mono Lake, California

The Great Basin region is one of "washboard" topography, created by alternating high mountain ranges and intervening valleys stretching eastward from the Sierra Nevada and Cascade ranges. The streams of the Great Basin do not drain into the ocean; instead, they lose themselves in arid basins or collect in inland seas, referred to as lakes. These are among California's most productive ecosystems. Waterfowl, shorebirds, and grebes descend on inland seas such as Mono, Goose, Middle, and Honey lakes to rest and feed during their migratory journeys, and they depend on these lakes for breeding sites.

40

When the icy grip of winter puts its hold on the Great Basin, many of the birds and mammals migrate to more suitable habitats. The enterprising muskrat, however, is active in the streams and lakes of the Great Basin all winter, even under the ice. Thick fur conserves its body heat and keeps cold water away from its skin as it forages underwater or on the surface for cattails and other aquatic plants. Winter is a time of stress, for the ice allows predators such as coyotes to penetrate the muskrat's marshy domain.

Pintail Ducks, Tule Lake, Klamath Basin, California

It has long been presumed that geese and swans mate for life, but that ducks seek new mates each season. Coming upon a pair of pintail ducks frozen in the ice, however, one wonders about the cause of such a tragedy. Did a sudden drop in temperature catch two healthy ducks unaware?

Were both male and female sick and unable to flee? Or did a healthy bird stay with a sick or hurt mate at the cost of its own life?

Alabama Hills, Sierra Nevada, California

4 :: THE SIERRA NEVADA

With its rugged topography, unequaled resources, and superb communities of flora and fauna, the majestic Sierra Nevada is a dominant feature of California, offering a variety of climatic conditions and environmental and biological features characteristic of the entire spectrum available from northern Mexico to the fringes of the Arctic Circle.

John Muir often referred to the Sierra Nevada as "the cathedral of light." The range is an open cordillera, with extensive meadows and white granite faces planed off by past glaciers. Originally, much of the forest on the west slope facing the Central Valley consisted of enormous trees, widely spaced, with little brushy undergrowth. The giant sequoias are best known, of course, but they were highly local in distribution, between Yosemite and Sequoia National Park at midelevations. An investigation of the spotty distribution of big trees found that they were clustered in areas plotted by Forest Service fire lookouts as being of great attraction to lightning strikes. Presumably the lightning started frequent ground fires that exposed mineral soil required for sequoia seedlings to become established. The lightning fires, plus those started by aborigines, maintained the open "cathedral" aspect of the forests on the western slope, consisting not only of sequoia but also of magnificent boles of yellow pine, sugar pine, and red fir. As noted by many early visitors, brush and tree reproduction were infrequent.

The higher, exposed reaches of the mountains have always been open, but the forest zone has been greatly modified. Beginning with the Gold Rush, logging removed most of the mature timber, making way for dense stands of shrubs and young trees. The logging slash and vigorous new growth supplied fuel for destructive wildfires of a sort rarely experienced in the primeval forest. Subsequent effective forest fire prevention has permitted proliferation of heavy ground cover and forest reproduction, even in national parks and other areas that were not logged. These sequential changes in woody vegetation have altered the habitat for wildlife populations occupying the Sierra forests. The mule deer serves to illustrate the point.

The mountain men and pioneers who explored the Sierra Nevada in the early 1800s found abundant deer in the western foothills, but relatively few deer in the upper reaches of the range or on the eastern slope. The foothill deer were a resident population of the nonmigratory black-tailed race of mule deer. They apparently thrived in the oak parklands and foothill riparian strips described so graphically by Frémont. The migratory deer that summer in the high country and drop down to intermediate levels in winter (3,000 to 5,000 feet on the western slope) were scarce because brush species needed for their winter forage were not abundant in the mature forest at that level. However, when the forest was logged and burned, brushfields in profusion sprang up, supplying abundant and nutritious winter food on which the migratory deer could thrive. On the western slope some of the principal browse species were buck brush and deer brush (two species of *Ceanothus*) and mountain mahogany (*Cercocarpus*). On the east slope the most important browse was bitterbrush (*Purshia*), a key winter deer food.

Persistent overhunting kept deer populations at a low level from 1850 to about 1920, but with effective legal protection, deer proliferated rapidly thereafter to fill the niche inadvertently created for them by slash-and-burn forestry. Migratory herds on both slopes of the Sierra reached peak levels in the 1940s; deer hunters were happy, and government wildlife agencies proudly took credit. But ecologic balances can be notably unstable, and the sequential stages of plant succession that gave rise to good deer range advanced to engulf the browse plants in the closing canopy of a maturing young forest. Loss of the nutritive forage plants was considerably hastened by the high numbers of deer themselves, which overbrowsed the most palatable species both on the winter ranges and in the high country where they migrated to rear their fawns. Additional grazing by domestic livestock compounded the problem. In the 1960s and 1970s deer numbers steadily declined to a level about one-third that of the peak years.

The changes in forest cover that governed deer numbers had an equal impact on other animals. Species such as the pileated woodpecker were very much at home in the primeval mature forest. Snag tops of old trees offered sites for nest cavities and foraging grounds for the big birds to seek wood-boring insects. Replacement of most of the tall timber with brush fields and young forest left scant pileated woodpecker habitat. Similarly, pine martens and fishers utilized tall dense forest as one habitat component, and their numbers dropped to a very low level as a result of logging, combined with persistent overtrapping. Now the marten population is again increasing, and the fisher is reoccupying some localities in northern California. In 1937 Joseph Grinnell reported that their larger relative the wolverine, whose home is the higher reaches of the mountains, was limited to a mere handful of survivors in the vicinity of Sequoia National Park. Protection from trapping permitted an increase in numbers and a spread of occupied range to encompass the whole Sierra Nevada and the Cascades from northwestern California on into Oregon.

The beaver, which originally was practically nonexistent on the west slope of the Sierra Nevada and was completely absent on the east slope, profited greatly by the destruction of the mature forest and the intrusion of hardwood second growth, especially aspen. Beavers depend on foods such as aspen and willow for winter sustenance, and they responded in numbers as these plants proliferated. Today beavers are widespread and abundant on both slopes.

The upper reaches of the Sierra Nevada, where the wolverine again wanders, are the areas favored by backpackers and wilderness lovers. In midsummer, when the mosquitoes have largely disappeared and the weather is consistently pleasant, the high Sierra is indeed a delightful pleasure ground. The meadows are lush green, dotted with colorful wildflowers. Marmots bask on sunny boulders. Chipmunks and golden-mantled ground squirrels scuttle about popular campsites, picking up crumbs dropped by previous campers. On talus slopes the industrious pikas are curing hay and storing it deep among the rocks for winter. Horned larks and rosy finches are feeding their newly fledged young. And the glassy surface of a nearby lake may be dimpled by rising trout. It is no wonder that thousands upon thousands of visitors shoulder their packs and hike into the Sierra each summer.

The heavy foot-traffic has its adverse effects, however. Shy mountain dwellers such as the bighorn sheep seem to avoid human disturbance, and this may have contributed to problems in the recovery of the sheep population. In 1950 there were estimated to be 390 Sierra

Yellow-Bellied Marmot, Sage Hen Creek, Sierra Nevada, California

The yellow-bellied marmot, largest member of the ground squirrel family, builds up layers of fat during the summer and fall. When the first snow falls, marmots merely crowd into shelters among the rocks and boulders and remain there throughout the winter in hibernation.

bighorns, occurring in five bands between Convict Creek and Olancha Peak. In 1980, after thirty years of complete protection from hunting, only 247 bighorns could be found, in two bands. Although the Forest Service created a zoological preserve where hikers were instructed to stay on trails to minimize contact with the bighorns, habitat factors such as quality of winter range are probably more important in inhibiting the recovery of this bighorn population. Other problems associated with excessive numbers of recreationists are trail and meadow deterioration, campsite trampling, pollution of waters, and exhaustion of firewood. It has become necessary to regulate numbers of visitors to the high Sierra through a permit system.

Another mammal that interacts with summer visitors is the black bear. Centers of bear concentration are Yosemite and Sequoia/Kings Canyon National Parks. There, bears are not hunted, and many become bold and unafraid, finding that people have in their camps and vehicles food items that are highly attractive to the bear palate. Persistent bears become serious and dangerous pests in campgrounds, and when they are trapped and moved to distant points in the high country, they turn their attention to backpackers' camps. The objective of managing bears in the Sierra Nevada is to keep them out in the woods eating natural foods. To achieve this goal, incorrigible "camp bums" have to be actively discouraged or, failing that, destroyed.

The black bear is a true omnivore, eating a surprising variety of plant and animal products. Mast foods such as manzanita berries, pine nuts, and acorns are staples; carrion, small mammals, and insects are preferred sources of protein. In spring a few bears learn to canvass the meadows for newborn fawns. One study in the Sequoia area disclosed that a primary summer food was yellowjackets and their grubs, dug up from underground nests.

Summer bird life in the Sierra is rich in variety and abundance. As the snow retreats, and flowers and greenery emerge to cloak the meadows and hillsides, wave on wave of migratory birds return from winter quarters to their mountain breeding grounds. Warblers, vireos, and flycatchers flit through creekside willows or the topmost branches of the pines, flashing their colors and gleaning newly emerged insects.

The tremendous diversity of wildlife in the California mountains is due to the great range of physical conditions. Many species of plants and animals are so sensitive to physical factors such as light, moisture, and temperature that they can exist only within a narrow zone where conditions are optimum. Climbing a mountain, we notice the zonation of plants and animals according to altitude and, therefore, temperature. These life zones or belts are rarely abrupt; rather, the zones overlap and mix, one merging gradually into the next. On a very steep slope, however, where changes in exposure are more dramatic, the boundaries between two adjacent life zones become more distinct and pronounced.

Eastern Slope, Sierra Nevada, California

Tree swallows dip over aspen patches seeking woodpecker holes for their nest cavities. Juncos and sparrows forage on the ground or in low shrubs. Robins tilt their heads listening for worms in the sod, and spotted sandpipers and dippers patrol the streams. Each dawn brings a medley of birdsong as individual males proclaim their territorial holdings and serenade their actual or potential mates. But very shortly the mating game is over, eggs hatch, and parent birds—male as well as female—are caught up in the responsibility of feeding hungry young. The volume of birdsong drops nearly to zero as the demands of parenthood increase. Finally, young birds are fledged, the adults start to molt their worn feathers, and another breeding season is over. Small insectivorous birds of many species form loose flocks that drift through the forest canopy, feeding as they go in silence or emitting faint cheeps. As summer wanes and the first cold nights dust the meadows with frost, the migratory birds will be gone, their departure as silent and inconspicuous as their arrival was noisy and advertised.

Some birds do not migrate but instead have developed strategies for surviving a Sierra winter. One of these is the blue grouse—a stout fowl of the conifer forest. In spring the cocks hoot from the tops of tall trees to attract females, with whom they rendezvous on the ground for mating. The hens then nest and rear their chicks without help from the cocks, who have wandered up the mountain in company of male friends. During the summer all the grouse feed on berries and the tender leaves of ground-hugging plants. When winter arrives, the birds fly up into fir trees (usually white fir) and settle there for the whole winter, feeding solely on fir needles. This poor-quality food sustains the grouse in good health only because the bird's intestinal tract contains a rich mix of bacteria and protozoa that digest the cellulose in the needles, yielding simple sugars that the grouse can assimilate. Both microbes and grouse profit from this symbiotic relationship.

Other wintering birds include woodpeckers, chickadees, nuthatches, and creepers that find insects in trees, and Steller's jays and Clark's crows that seek the seeds in conifer cones. Some years cone crops fail, in which case the jays and crows live precariously or desert the Sierra altogether, showing up in foothills or in distant areas (even in the Coast Ranges) seeking food.

The blue grouse was once thought to hibernate during winter because it is so seldom seen after the first heavy snows. Most animals and birds in mountainous regions move to lower elevations with the arrival of low temperatures and deep snow, but the blue grouse either moves higher and higher up the slopes to find food and cover in the fir trees or remains where it is in subalpine forests.

Blue Grouse, Sierra Nevada, California

Most of the hawks that winter in the Central Valley nest in the Sierra or farther to the north and east. Among the most effective of predators on birds is the Cooper's hawk. This abundant medium-sized accipiter nests in a dense tree and hunts by flying low and fast over the forest floor, pouncing on any prey it can surprise on the ground. Birds and small mammals such as chipmunks and ground squirrels are electrified by the sudden appearance of a marauding Cooper's hawk, fleeing in terror if they have time, or "freezing" if they do not. The goshawk is a larger version of the same ilk, capable of mastering prey up to the size of blue grouse and young marmots. These two super-predators patrol most of the Sierra and keep the smaller vertebrates on their toes.

The diminutive kestrel, or sparrow hawk, which is actually a true falcon, nests in tree cavities, preferably near open meadows and sparse brushfields where it can hunt grasshoppers and lizards. Male kestrels return to the Sierra foothills and establish territories in anticipation of the arrival of the females. After a female checks out a male's property and selects an appropriate nest cavity, she settles there and lets the male feed her while she lays a clutch of eggs and incubates them to hatching. Thereafter, for a time, the male is feeding not only the female but also the young. Since grasshoppers are a primary prey, and since they are not active until midmorning, the male has to supply some more substantial food to quiet hungry mouths in the early morning hours. This is accomplished by bringing the female a vertebrate, such as a mouse, a small bird, or a lizard, which she caches in a tree near the nest. Then at daylight both she and the young can feed until the overworked male can begin his daily shuttle of grasshoppers.

The small mammals are not equipped to migrate and so must endure the winter in one way or another. Many of the rodents hibernate in underground burrows, living on the fat accumulated during summer. By lowering their body temperatures and reducing metabolism to the very edge of death, the marmots, chipmunks, and ground squirrels can coast through the winter months, emerging in the spring gaunt and hungry but still alive. Some of their close relatives take a more cavalier attitude toward the vicissitudes of cold weather and scramble for a living in the trees or under the snow. The sassy, noisy chickaree,

Golden trout are at home in the high-elevation streams and lakes of the Kern River drainage system in the southern Sierra Nevada. Winter snows cover the trout's habitat, forcing it to feed on plankton and larvae. Later in the season, holes open up in the ice, and welcoming a change of diet, golden trout jump vigorously at surface insects, often landing on ice floes.

Golden Trout, Cottonwood Basin, Southern Sierra Nevada, California

or Douglas squirrel, prepares for the ordeal by cutting and piling conifer cones into middens or caches and drawing on these stored supplies for the whole winter's food. A typical midden consists of a pile of thousands of cones stacked against the base of a pine or fir tree. Even in times of deep snow, the animal can dig down to its larder and carry a cone up the tree to shuck out the seeds at leisure.

Flying squirrels follow a different pattern, gnawing the bark off the upper boles of lodgepole pines to eat the cambium layer. The tree responds to this affront by producing scar tissue, which, it turns out, is even better food for flying squirrels than the original cambium. The squirrel thus draws sustenance from the tree, the gnawing leading finally to girdling of the top and production of a snag, which then has attractions for woodpeckers. Porcupines similarly mistreat yellow pines, with comparable unsatisfactory results from the standpoint of the tree and the forester.

In the meadows, the mountain vole, or meadow mouse, creates a network of tunnels under the snow that serve as transport lanes to clumps of grass, the vole's winter food. Each mouse builds a snug nest of dry grass on the ground surface, insulated from above by snow. This cozy winter arrangement would be ideal except for the presence in the same meadow of an ermine, or short-tailed weasel, of the same diameter as the vole. The weasel probes the snow until it penetrates the mouse's tunnels, which it follows easily, straight to the nest; it kills and eats the mouse and takes over the nest as its own. Working out of this base for a period of days, the weasel may capture and kill all the neighboring voles, dragging them back to the "home" nest to eat. When the snow melts in spring, the weasel is gone, but one can find the exposed mouse nests, one of which is thickly lined with gray mouse fur. Outside the nest, neatly piled by the entrance, are the jaws of all the voles brought there for consumption, along with a collection of weasel droppings. The melancholy remains attest to the shortness of life among meadow voles.

A. Starker Leopold
April 1983

High mountain meadows surrounded by forest are extremely important to wildlife. Meadows create a border, an edge effect, allowing two distinct habitats to merge. Because open meadows are free of snow long before the shaded forests, plants requiring light and moisture thrive in them, in turn becoming important sources of sustenance during late spring for wildlife such as this mule deer doe. Few animals are restricted to either meadow or forest, and there is much movement back and forth.

Mule Deer, Sierra Nevada, California

White-Faced Ibis, Los Banos, San Joaquin Valley, California

5 :: THE CENTRAL VALLEY

As the afternoon sun plunges behind the Coast Range in the west, evening settles upon the San Joaquin Valley. Silhouetted against the last light of day, a flock of white-faced ibis is feeding, their downward-curving bills probing for invertebrates in the soft mud. These birds are colonial in their nesting habits; large numbers of them build homes close together, each pair making a nest platform of broken tules. The graceful white-faced ibis, here illustrating so elegantly the beauty and tranquility of open space, is one of many species whose survival is linked to the survival of the large freshwater marshes of the San Joaquin Valley.

On a hot summer day the floor of the Central Valley is a shimmering mirage. Neither the Sierra Nevada to the east nor the Coast Range to the west can be clearly perceived through the haze. Rich fields stretching for miles across the Valley floor are the veritable breadbasket of California agriculture. In the southern San Joaquin the dominant crop is cotton; in the Sacramento to the north, rice is dominant. But interspersed are varied plantings, including corn, tomatoes, sugar beets, wheat, barley, vineyards, and many kinds of orchards. Most of these crops require irrigation, so the fields are bordered by a complex network of ditches and channels that draw water from the streams flowing off adjoining highlands (mostly from the Sierra Nevada) and apply it as needed to the thirsty tilled soils. The summer haze in the Valley derives largely from evaporating irrigation water.

No region of California has been so completely altered from its original condition as the Central Valley. In its own way it is an interesting place now, but the pristine landscape must have been strikingly beautiful, according to the accounts of many early visitors. Among these, Frémont was perhaps the most lyrical and the most precise in his description of the country in 1844. He led an exploratory military expedition that traveled south from Oregon to the Truckee River, thence wandering rather aimlessly over the Sierra in midwinter and finally descending the American River to Sutter's Fort, east of Sacramento. Doubtless the hardship of the mountain crossing enhanced the charm of the Valley in springtime, but the place certainly made an impression on Frémont. He speaks glowingly of oak woodland or savanna, with little bands of deer seen under the oaks among wildflowers and grasses: "From the upland we descended into broad groves on the river, consisting of the evergreen [live oak], and a new species of a white-oak [valley oak], with a large tufted top, and three to six feet in diameter. Among these was no brushwood; and the grassy surface gave to it the appearance of parks in an old-settled country. . . . We hurried on, the valley being gay with flowers and some of the banks being absolutely golden with the California poppy."

After a period of recovery and reoutfitting at Sutter's, Frémont led his party south, skirting the foothills of the Sierra and crossing in turn the Cosumnes, Mukelemnes [sic], Calaveras, Stanislaus, Tuolumne, and Merced rivers, describing repeatedly the riparian woodland that paralleled each stream. (Virtually none of this riparian vegetation is left today.) The plains became progressively more arid and sandy as the party proceeded southward, and the filaree (*Erodium*), which Frémont noted grew two to three feet high in moist sites, was only two to three inches in height on the dry hill slopes of the southeastern San Joaquin Valley. The great interior Tulare Lake was full to overflowing in 1844, and the party had to detour to the east of it. From various ponds and water bodies the party disturbed "multitudes of wild fowl, principally geese." Likewise, elk were abundant in the "tulares" (bulrushes), and antelope were seen daily on the open plains. Surprisingly, wild horses were present in substantial herds, especially on the west side of the San Joaquin River. They derived, apparently, from stock escaping the early Spanish missions. Such was the original scene in central California as observed by an appreciative traveler.

At an earlier date, the Spanish had established their missions and haciendas along the California coast, and although their cattle and horses proliferated and spread to the Valley, neither the friars nor the vaqueros made any attempt to settle far inland from the cool coast. Mountain men in quest of beaver were the first Caucasians to exploit the Valley riches. Jedediah Smith, Alexander McLeod, Peter Ogden, and John Work were among the pioneers who came for furs. In the 1830s the wealth of beaver and otter in the Central Valley became known, and parties of British, Russian, French Canadian, and American trappers competed to skim the rich harvest.

In 1832 John Work led a party of over one hundred men, women, and children from Hudson's Bay Company headquarters at Fort Vancouver across central Oregon to the headwaters of the Sacramento River and

In some places, luxuriant jungles of oak, sycamore, ash, willow, alder, walnut, poplar, and wild grape still form dense, impenetrable walls of undisturbed riparian woodland along both banks of the Sacramento River, supplying food and cover for a wide variety of wildlife.

Riparian Forest, Sacramento River, California

down the Central Valley as far as the Stanislaus River. Work's diary gives an accurate record of numbers of beaver trapped, numbers of deer and elk killed for food, problems with Indians, and sickness in his party, but he tells very little about the country. Still, from the record of animals taken, much can be surmised. One area where elk and deer were especially abundant was the vicinity of Marysville Buttes. Work stated: "We have been a month here and we could not have fallen on a better place to pass a part of the dead winter season when nothing could be done in the way of trapping on account of the height of the waters. There was excellent feeding for the horses and abundance of animals for the people to subsist on; 395 elk, 148 deer, 17 bears, and 8 antelopes have been killed in a month." In some mountain areas, however, game was scarce and the party suffered. In 1833 the party returned to Fort Vancouver with 1,023 beaver and otter skins. Other trapping expeditions followed one after another for about ten years, at which time the easily available furs had largely been taken. When gold was discovered along the American River in 1848, the trickle of explorers and settlers increased to a torrent. The California wilderness came to an instant and spectacular end.

Hungry miners and newly arrived settlers desperately needed meat. The supply of Spanish cattle was soon exhausted, and wildlife of the Valley and adjoining foothills became the obvious next source. The meat of the grizzly bear was highly prized, and its numbers were quickly thinned to the point of oblivion by commercial hunters such as the notorious Grizzly Adams. Similarly, deer, antelope, and tule elk—the other large game species that were so abundant in the 1830s and 1840s—were soon extinct or virtually so. William Brewer, writing of the vicinity of Mount Diablo in 1861, stated: "Game was once very abundant—bear in the hills, and deer, antelope and elk like cattle in herds. [A local settler] said he had known a party of thirty or forty [horsemen] to lasso twenty-eight elk in one Sunday. All are now exterminated, but we find their horns by the Hundreds."

Commercial hunting of waterfowl started when the larger game species were gone. Valley lowlands and marshes, totaling probably 5 million acres, attracted uncountable clouds of ducks, geese, and swans, and hunting entrepreneurs were quick to take advantage of the

The pristine grasslands of the San Joaquin Valley once attracted great herds of pronghorn antelope and tule elk; though the antelope have disappeared, a few small bands of elk can be found. The smallest of the elk of North America, the tule elk is native only to California where it formerly ranged throughout the great Central Valley, migrating from the valley floor to the adjacent foothills when flooding occurred. To hear the bugling and see the jousting of bull tule elk in the fall is an experience equaled perhaps only by catching a glimpse of newborn tule elk calves in the springtime.

Tule Elk, San Joaquin Valley, California

greedy market. With armaments of many types, including punt guns and large-bore shotguns, these nimrods supplied the San Francisco trade with thousands of prime birds. Officers of the California Fish and Game Commission estimated that 350,000 ducks and upwards of 20,000 geese were marketed in California in the winter of 1911–12, and by then commercial bags were decreasing precipitously, presumably because of decreasing numbers of birds.

In 1916 the United States and Canada signed the Migratory Bird Treaty, which, among other things, made commercialization of waterfowl illegal. After the U.S. Senate ratified this treaty in 1918, the federal government entered the field of waterfowl conservation. Federal and state wildlife agencies, working together, undertook to enforce the legislation intended to protect the breeding stocks of migratory game birds. Illegal commercial taking of wild ducks continued for twenty years or so, especially in the Central Valley, but law and order finally prevailed and market hunting essentially ceased.

But then another, more serious, factor came to prejudice the welfare of marsh wildlife—the cumulative drainage of wetlands for agriculture. As early as the 1930s it was recognized that the most important continental breeding grounds for waterfowl were shrinking under the impact of agricultural drainage. The prairies of the northern United States and south central Canada had long been known as the "duck factory" of the continent, and government agencies plus a private foundation called Ducks Unlimited have invested great effort and millions of dollars in purchasing or leasing waterfowl breeding marshes to preserve them from drainage. Additional refuges were created along the migratory flyways and on the wintering grounds, including seventeen state and federal areas in the Central Valley. Today the remaining marshlands in central California constitute only 300,000 acres, or about 6 percent of the original wetlands. One-third of this area is in government refuges, two-thirds in private ranches and duck clubs. This residue of habitat for transient and wintering water birds is proving to be inadequate, and the future of many species is insecure.

But despite the reduced areas of wetlands, the concentration of wildlife in the remaining California marshes is seasonally spectacular. On Gray Lodge Waterfowl Area near Gridley, for example, there will be

The male wood duck has often been described as the most beautiful and brightly marked American duck. Although lacking the brilliant coloration of her mate, the female, with her white eye-ring and stripe behind the eye, displays more color than the females of most other species. Wood ducks frequent the secluded, slow-moving, timber-bordered streams and freshwater sloughs of the Sacramento and San Joaquin valleys.

Wood Ducks, Sacramento River, California

upward of a million ducks and twenty thousand geese on a weekend in December when most of the migrants have arrived from the north. Species like the pintail and mallard have learned to spend the daylight hours safely loafing on one or another of the refuges and then flying out at dusk to feed on grain dropped to the ground during the process of harvest. Rice, corn, kafir, and safflower are favorite stubble foods. Before daylight most of the well-fed birds return to their sanctuaries, effectively eluding the hunters' guns. Similarly, widgeon and the several species of geese loaf in the refuges and cruise out to the fields of clover or winter grain to graze on green foods, which they prefer. In this manner, waterfowl in the Central Valley of California make it through most winters until it is time to migrate northward again to the traditional breeding grounds.

However, in dry winters Valley farmers take every opportunity to plow under the stubbles left from the previous growing season, thus preparing the seedbed for the new year. Plowed stubbles offer little or no food for hungry ducks, and the marshland foods are generally exhausted long before spring. This leaves the birds underfed and in poor shape to migrate hundreds of miles north and to nest and produce healthy young. A dry winter, in other words, is a time of crisis for those species of Valley ducks whose habit it is to winter on crop residues. Marsh-feeding species that do not fly out to grain are equally disadvantaged when the pintails and mallards are forced to glean their living in the marsh, competing directly with the teal, shovelers, gadwalls, and diving ducks that ordinarily seek their whole livelihood in the wetlands. These vicissitudes of life for waterfowl are not immediately evident to the admiring visitor who with camera and binoculars comes to watch the magnificent panorama of birds on a refuge.

Ducks and geese are not the only migratory birds that require wetlands for their winter habitat. Marsh birds such as herons, egrets, bitterns, and rails add interest and beauty to the bogs and bayous of the Central Valley. Some of the smallest of these, such as the diminutive sora rail, make astonishingly long migrations from breeding grounds in southern Canada. A sora, flushed from the marsh, flutters into the air with apparent labor, and after a flight of fifty yards or so flops down as though exhausted. One gets the impression that this little bird

The mallard is a common resident in suitable localities throughout California, nesting in coastal marshlands, the rivers and ponds of the Central Valley, and the mountain lakes of the Sierra Nevada. The storms that move through the Pacific Northwest cause the numbers of mallards in the Central Valley to be greatly augmented during the winter season by migrants from the north.

Mallard Ducks, Sacramento Valley, California

can scarcely fly. And yet the evidence of its seasonal appearance and disappearance belies that conclusion. All rails, including the sora and the common coot, migrate at night and thereby escape the depredations of hawks, which surely could overtake such slow-flying prey during daylight hours.

Presumably the shrinkage of Valley wetlands has had a depressing effect on the numbers of marsh birds, as in the case of waterfowl. And yet the shorebirds (or at least some species of them) seem to have adapted with considerable success to changed patterns of land use. The handsome long-billed curlew, for example, thrives in pastures and hay meadows that produce insects and invertebrates in abundance. Joseph Grinnell stated in 1918 in his classic volume on California game birds that this curlew had been greatly reduced by commercial hunting, winter flocks of two to twenty birds being normal; today, under complete protection from shooting, the curlew is to be seen in winter flocks of thousands. Jacksnipe, dowitchers, and many sandpipers and "peeps" find suitable winter habitat in stubbles and pastures soggy with winter rain. Stilts and avocets nest locally in the Central Valley, and their numbers are augmented in winter by migrants. Even the stately sandhill cranes gather in the San Joaquin Valley in great winter flocks, finding sustenance in the grain stubbles of foothill ranches. Both the shorebirds and the cranes were severely overhunted for the commercial market in the early years of the century, but with protection of the Migratory Bird Treaty Act, they quickly recovered, to occupy such favorable habitats as remain in the Valley.

One of the delights of Valley birdwatchers is the parade of hawks that winter there. Cooper's hawks, marsh hawks, red-tails, rough-legs, and kestrels all congregate in the flatlands, which are snow-free and suitable for finding prey. Rarely, a prairie falcon or a golden eagle will be seen. In November, as winter envelops the mountains and the northland, these visitors appear in increasing numbers, peaking in January and February. As spring approaches they follow the retreating snowline back toward the traditional nesting areas. The one abundant resident hawk of the Valley—the dainty white-tailed kite—puts up with this seasonal intrusion into its hunting grounds, though now and then kites will be seen diving on a red-tail or rough-leg in a fit of

California's remaining native wetlands are remarkable for the concentration of birds found in them. These birds have developed specialized bills, legs, and feet that enable them to forage effectively throughout their habitat. Included in this group are shorebirds such as the long-billed curlews and common snipes, as well as greater and lesser sandhill cranes, white pelicans, and black-necked stilts.

Long-Billed Curlews, Los Banos, San Joaquin Valley, California

pique. At one period early in the 1900s, white-tailed kites were so rare in California that they were put on the completely protected list along with the sea otter and the condor. But their numbers have recouped spectacularly, and now they are among the more abundant raptors, even in winter.

The marshland mammals have also demonstrated adaptive resilience. The abundance of beavers in the Valley marshes attracted the mountain men of the 1830s and 1840s, who in a short time reduced the animal to relative scarcity. By the period of general settlement in California, beavers were so scarce as to be almost nonexistent. After the beaver hat (the Abe Lincoln topper) went out of style, and the value of pelts dropped precipitously, there were only enough animals left to constitute a skeleton breeding population. This situation continued until 1911, when for the first time beavers were given legal protection in California. The population in the Central Valley began a steady recovery, and in 1921 Joseph Grinnell estimated that one thousand of the animals existed. A few years later, in 1925, the numbers had reached a level where beavers constituted a problem to Valley farmers, undermining levees, damming irrigation ditches, and cutting down fruit trees. Legal trapping was resumed, raising fears of complete eradication. But the beaver has persisted handsomely in the Valley to this day, foraging on willows and cottonwoods that spring up on river banks and levees.

A second aquatic mammal that has thrived under legal protection is the river otter. Like the beaver, it was severely overtrapped in the Valley but has come back astonishingly in recent years. The area of greatest abundance now, as in early times, is the Sacramento–San Joaquin delta and the Suisun Marsh. It is commonplace today to see this graceful animal bobbing in the water or sliding down a slippery bank in gay abandon. Families tend to remain together, a female with two or three young being a common grouping. There are records of male parents helping to lead and care for young, although this is not a common attribute of mustelid mammals. Otters eat mostly fish and crayfish, with a few frogs and insects for variety.

In the Sacramento Valley, large and small streams fringed with vegetation break up the landscape. At one time, these winding ribbons of foliage extended from the base of the Sierra Nevada and Coast Range foothills all the way to the Sacramento River and its adjacent wetlands. This riparian habitat supports a greater variety of wildlife than any other type of habitat found in California. Just one example of the countless animals that make the riparian zone their home is the ringtailed cat, a carnivore of such retiring habits that it is rarely seen.

Ringtail, Sacramento River, California

The third abundant aquatic mammal, the muskrat, is alien to the Central Valley but was introduced inadvertently when some enterprising farmer imported this exotic to start a fur farm. Of course the fence fell down and a few rats escaped into an ideal habitat for colonization. Today muskrats in the Valley probably number in the millions, and each winter trappers take many thousands of prime pelts for the commercial market. Ranchers encourage trapping, since muskrats are an unmitigated pest, burrowing through levees and rice checks. The nutria, closely related to the muskrat, is another alien that has a foothold in the San Joaquin Valley and is spreading northward. It is bigger than the muskrat and will dig bigger holes in levees.

Among the other mammalian residents of the Valley are the ringtailed cat, the raccoon, the striped skunk, and the San Joaquin kit fox. The ringtail was thought of as a desert species, and indeed it does occur there. But its abundance on wooded riverbanks and in valley swales came to light when large numbers of nesting boxes were mounted in trees for the use of wood ducks; on investigation many of the boxes were found to harbor ringtailed cats instead. Not that anyone objected, for these beautiful little prowlers of the night are welcome predators of pest rodents. As for raccoons, they also are nocturnal; their presence is readily detected by tracks in the mud. Skunks proclaim their association in the Valley ecosystem by gentle odor wafted on the evening breeze. The diminutive kit fox frequents the arid shrublands of the southern Valley; its habitat shrinks with every acre that is brought under irrigation. In the 1970s a population of red foxes mysteriously appeared in the lower Sacramento Valley near the Marysville Buttes. Although this species occurs sparingly in the Sierra Nevada, it had not been known in the lowlands for many years. It is considered possible that this new emergence may be traced to introduction of the eastern red fox by some houndsman who thrills to the baying of a blue-tick hound, for the red fox is the classic quarry of the pack.

One exotic that definitely has found a home in the Central Valley is the ring-necked pheasant. This adaptable species was brought to Europe from Asia by Marco Polo and is a favorite game bird there now. In western North America the pheasant was imported directly from China by Judge O. N. Denny, U.S. consul-general in Shanghai. In 1881

The San Joaquin Valley was once a vast sea of grass inhabited by a tremendous number of diverse creatures. Today, with California's tremendous population growth and accompanying economic and agricultural development, the grasslands are greatly reduced, as are the populations of animals dependent on them for survival. The San Joaquin kit fox is among the creatures characteristic of the grasslands, along with the burrowing owl, the blunt-nosed leopard lizard, and the rattlesnake.

San Joaquin Kit Fox, Buena Vista Valley, California

Mr. Denny sent a crate of pheasants by ship to his brother in Oregon, who released them on the family farm in the Willamette Valley. The birds proved to be amazingly well adapted to that habitat, and within a few years they had increased to the point where a legal hunting season was declared. Soon thereafter other states, including California, imported the bird, and its range spread through most of the irrigated farmlands in the West. This handsome foreigner is now a primary game species in the Central Valley, where it thrives, particularly in rice-growing localities.

Considering the extent to which the Central Valley has been modified by agriculture and human occupancy, the array of wildlife that still finds habitat there is rather surprising. Today a few black-tailed deer have reinvaded the Valley in willow thickets bordering sloughs and canals, and even the native tule elk has been introduced on two waterfowl refuges—San Luis Island near Los Banos and Grizzly Island in the Suisun Marsh. Yet as land use further intensifies, wildlife numbers will inevitably shrink. Agricultural efficiency demands larger and larger fields to justify the use of larger and more expensive machinery. To make fields larger and more amenable to machine cultivation and harvest, fence rows are removed, low spots are drained and filled with a land plane, and woodlands are cleared. It is precisely these fence rows, low swales, and woodlands that offer habitat to many wild birds and mammals, however. So both the variety and the abundance of wildlife in the Central Valley are declining and will continue to do so as agriculture becomes more mechanized.

A. Starker Leopold
April 1983

Huge valley oaks, a species unique to California, dot the fertile lowlands of the lower San Joaquin Valley. These oaks are not generally distributed in the San Joaquin, large portions of which are devoid of trees of any kind. Where these stately giants do occur, however, they are tremendously important to wildlife. Many birds use oaks for foraging, nesting, and perching, and several bird species regularly eat acorns. The valley oak shown hosts a great blue heron rookery, a pair of red-tailed hawks, and an egret.

Heron Rookery, San Luis Island, San Joaquin Valley, California

Shoveler Ducks, Los Banos, San Joaquin Valley, California

72

Ducks, geese, and swans are especially active at dawn and dusk, moving to and from their feeding grounds. During certain seasons, too, the swift-flying shoveler ducks are restless and spend much of the time on the wing.

Sutter Buttes and Butte Sink, Sacramento Valley, California

Just west of the majestic Sutter Buttes in the Sacramento Valley are ten thousand acres of natural wetlands known as the Butte Sink. The woodlands, seasonal wetlands, and permanently flooded marshes of the Butte Sink provide habitats for a variety of wildlife. The marshes, a natural overflow of the Sacramento River and Butte Creek, are among the most heavily used winter habitats for waterfowl migrating along the Pacific flyway.

Swainson's Hawk and Red-Winged Blackbird, San Luis Island, San Joaquin Valley, California

A bright summer day finds a red-winged blackbird up from its territory in the marsh, hoping to chase a Swainson's hawk a little farther down the road. The blackbird is a familiar inhabitant of the freshwater marshes of the San Joaquin Valley, but the Swainson's hawk is seldom seen. As riparian forests are cleared, grasslands al-

tered, and rodents poisoned, it has become difficult for this beautiful hawk to find food. The Swainson's hawk spends much of its time in willows and cottonwoods along rivers or sloughs. These trees serve as nesting sites and as convenient perches from which to scan the terrain for mice, moles, gophers, and ground squirrels.

White-Crowned Sparrows, Merced, San Joaquin Valley, California

The climate of the Central Valley attracts birds at all seasons of the year. The white-crowned sparrows winter amid the brush and thickets, moving to the high country for the summer breeding months. The yellow-billed cuckoo winters in South America, returning to the Central Valley for the summer. Black-crowned night herons live in the Valley all year round, resting by day and feeding by night.

Vernal Pool, Winter, San Joaquin Valley, California

Vernal pools, a phenomenon unique to California, are to be found in only a few areas of the grasslands of the San Joaquin Valley where a subsurface layer of clay or hardpan soil permits winter rains to form ponds that provide feeding and resting habitats for migratory waterfowl and shorebirds.

Vernal Pool, Spring, San Joaquin Valley, California

Winter gradually makes way for spring on the floor of the San Joaquin Valley. The heavy rains subside, leaving pools of standing water here and there. As the water slowly evaporates with the advancing warmer temperatures, successional rings of plants appear that are often endemic. These vernal, or springtime, pools and the floral rings they sustain constitute a delicate balance in nature.

Red-Winged Blackbird, Kern River, San Joaquin Valley, California

The warming and lengthening days of spring bring touches of green to the bare branches of willows in the marshes of the Central Valley. Here the male red-winged blackbird perches to display his richly colored epaulets and to sing his song, claim his territory, attract his mate, and herald the breeding season.

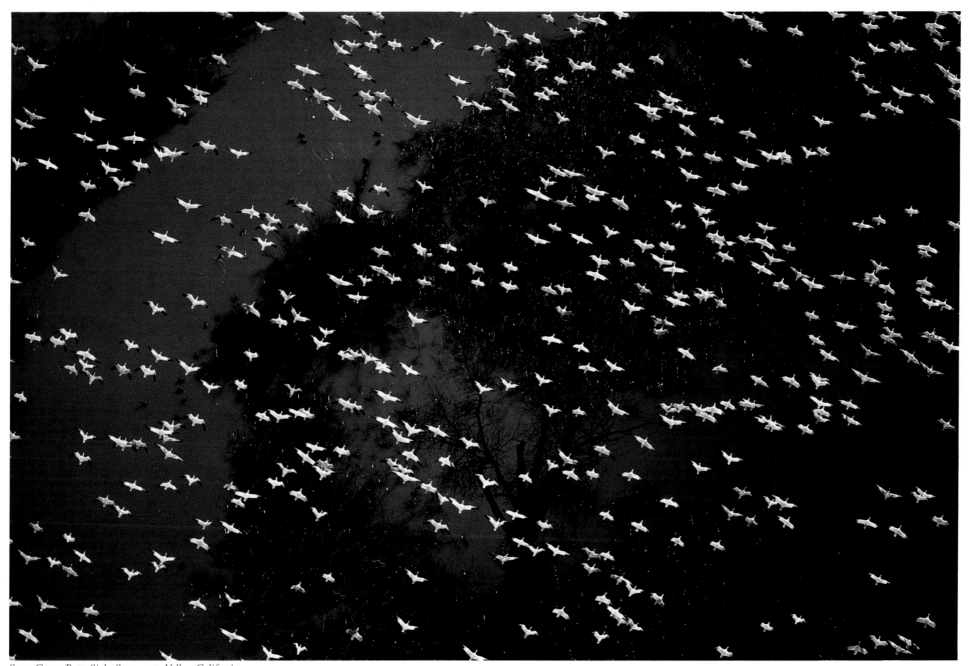

Snow Geese, Butte Sink, Sacramento Valley, California

The wetlands of the Sacramento Valley are an important factor in the lives of our waterfowl. It is in this ideal environment that wild ducks and geese spend their winters. Waterfowl such as the snow geese move through the Sacramento Valley in response to seasonal weather changes, food availability, and water conditions, but do so with greater difficulty each year as their winter habitat shrinks.

Santa Cruz Island, California

To most of the residents of the other forty-nine states, California consists of the coastal region from San Diego up through Los Angeles, San Francisco, and the Napa Valley. Most of the state goes unrecognized; what is interesting is the part where most of the people live—the big cities, the beaches, the freeways, and all the associated facilities that support more than twenty million Californians. This is also the original Spanish California. It was here that the missions, the pueblos, the presidios, and the ranchos of Spanish and Mexican settlers were located, the only part of California these settlers really knew. Not incidentally, it is the land favored by the typical California climate.

It is ironic in a way that most inhabitants of California, as well as most visitors to the state, have no real conception of coastal central and southern California. People are concentrated in the metropolitan areas, and freeways carry them from one urban area to another along fixed routes. They see what is visible from the road; the rest remains unknown. On a rare day in Los Angeles you can look from the city up into wilderness in the Sierra Madre. On a most unusual day, when the smog is away, one of the few surviving condors can climb up from its nest in the Los Padres National Forest and see out over the great conurbation of Los Angeles and its associated cities. City and wilderness are not far apart in southern California, thanks to the foresight of those who ringed the coastal plain with areas designated as national forest to be protected—forever, we hope—against urban expansion.

Farther north the wild is more extensive than the tamed. The people who struggle with traffic on U.S. Highway 101 rarely have time to notice the wild Santa Lucia Mountains off to the west, where elk and mountain lion still roam, and probably pay even less attention to the Cholame and Gabilan mountains to the east, which if not wilderness

The eight Channel Islands off the southern California coast are divided into two major groupings: the northern Channel Islands are San Miguel, Santa Rosa, Santa Cruz, and Anacapa; the southern Channel Islands are Santa Barbara, San Nicolas, Santa Catalina, and San Clemente. Each of these islands is the home of plants and animals found nowhere else in the world. Each has different features and landscapes, varying from low and sandy—like San Miguel Island—to high and wooded—like Santa Cruz Island.

81

are still basically wild range country. Even the San Francisco Bay cities are still ringed with country that is more natural than man-modified in the Diablo Range, Santa Cruz Mountains, and Marin hills. The coast itself, where gray whales swim off shore, and the sea lions and elephant seals pull up on rocks or beaches, still has long stretches where the only surfers wear feathers or fur and brush rabbits outnumber beach bunnies.

Starker Leopold had a longstanding interest in the wildlife of California as it existed when the state was first reached by European settlers and in the role wildlife played in the settlement of California. The Spanish explorers were not helpful in this respect, having been more interested in saving the souls of the Indians than in describing the natural scene. However, some wildlife truly impressed them. Foremost among such animals was the grizzly bear.

"Now one thing that I found surprising in reading the early history of the state," Leopold explained in a 1978 lecture, "was how important the grizzly bear was as a source of food. The meat was highly favored by everyone that used it. In later years when commercialization of game began, grizzly bear jerky brought about twice the price of jerky made from elk or deer or any of the other species. . . . The range of the grizzly was very similar to that of the black-tailed deer in that the high density zone was the coast and the Central Valley, not the Sierra and not at all in the desert. The grizzly bear, like the black-tailed deer, was an animal of the chaparral and oak woodland and hence was highly available to those parties that traveled up or down the coast. The deer, the elk, and the grizzly were probably the three main sources of food.

"The Spanish had a dreadful time with that grizzly when they had to deal with it with a rifle. They weren't very good with rifles, but they were with the *reata* [lariat]. One of the sports after the missions were established and the Spanish were well ensconced was to go out hunting grizzly bears with ropes . . . they would catch them and bring them in for their bear and bull fights.

"As the United States settlers came in they looked upon the grizzly initially as a source of food, secondly as a menace because it was a dangerous animal and hard on livestock. So [the bears] were rapidly shot

The ecosystem known as the Southern Interior Oak Woodland is reminiscent of the lands that made up the vast Spanish ranchos that once extended throughout the lush interior valleys of southern California. The dominant tree is the Engelmann oak, but the forest also includes the California live oak and the black oak. The oak woodlands are important to wildlife, for they provide food in the form of acorns and nest and den sites in trunks and branches. During inclement weather, the oak canopy forms a protective cover.

Southern Interior Oak Woodland, Santa Ysabel Valley, California

out. . . . One of the people that contributed most to the extermination of the grizzly bear was Grizzly Adams. I was amused to watch the television series about him where he is set up as a sort of St. Francis in buckskins. In point of fact he was one of the deadliest of hunters in California history. He spent all of his time shooting grizzly bears for the tallow, which was sold at very high prices, and for the meat.''

When Gaspar de Portolá led the first expedition to the San Francisco Bay in 1769–70, Leopold continued, "Pedro Fages was in charge of the troops. They had two divisions and great numbers of pack animals on which they loaded six months' supply of food. They were unable to get anything out of the country—they were lousy hunters and poor shots, apparently. When they reached the bay area they spoke frequently of how the soldiers were emaciated and hungry, and yet at the same time about the abundance of game they were seeing. The game they succeeded in killing was grizzly bears. The reason was that the grizzlies weren't afraid of anybody or anything, and they wouldn't run away. It so happened the first grizzly they encountered was somewhere down toward Los Angeles. He was a beautiful big fat bear and somebody killed him dead with one shot. He was delicious and they had a marvelous feast. The next one they found was skinny and about half dead. He was sick and wasn't very good eating, but they got the idea that these grizzlies were very simple and easy to kill. They later arrived at a valley near San Luis Obispo and saw sixteen of these bears together. They joyfully spurred their horses down and were going to shoot them up. They were shocked and a bit surprised when the bears came at them. Somehow they got out of the way without losing any soldiers, but they only killed one bear. Thereupon they became much more cautious about grizzly hunting.''

One animal that was to have a major influence on California settlement was the sea otter, an animal which at that time abounded along the entire California coast. These little otters had unusually dense, rich fur, which in the eighteenth and early nineteenth centuries sold for very high prices, particularly in China. The movement of the Spanish into California was undoubtedly expedited by the prospect that the Russians might take over a good share of the state in their pursuit of the sea otter trade. The Spanish in turn set up their own sea otter trade,

Wherever sea otters live, kelp forests thrive. This is because sea otters eat tremendous quantities of sea urchins, which feed on the kelp. The sea otter plays a key role in this ecosystem, for the kelp beds themselves serve as an important nursery for fish. The sea otter, in turn, derives benefit from the kelp beds. During storms, these animals find safety within the kelp, where the ocean surge is reduced. Female sea otters also wrap their young in kelp to anchor them to specific locations while the adult goes off to feed. While resting in kelp beds, sea otters conserve body heat by raising their forelegs and hind flippers from the water.

Southern Sea Otter, Point Lobos, California

shipping the skins to Canton by galleon. "They induced the native Indians to kill the otters for them, but the Indians did it reluctantly and did a poor job of skinning," Leopold noted in his lecture. "Nevertheless, the trade lasted for twenty years, from 1775 to 1795. As the Russians moved down, the Spanish attempted to accelerate their otter hunting and attempted to restrict the sale of otter skins so that only the priests could buy them. However, this did not last long, and after 1795 the Spanish were out of the otter business and the Russians definitely in it.

"The Russians established their bases at Sitka in 1804 and at Fort Ross north of San Francisco in 1812. By 1818 the Farallon Islands had become a base for otter hunting. They brought their own hunters, Aleuts with their skin boats. Really these Aleuts were forced into something akin to slavery, but they were marvelous otter hunters and far more efficient than the Spanish and the local Indians had been. Thereafter there were literally thousands of otter skins sent out, ultimately to reach the China market. The Russians exploited the sea otters until they became pretty hard to get. Meanwhile, the Mexicans tried to make it more difficult to hunt them, requiring complicated permits. In 1841 the Russians sold Fort Ross to John Sutter and left California. During the latter part of the Russian era, ships from New England and other nations joined in the trade. In 1810 one ship alone, the *O'Kane*, took out 5,456 otter skins. In 1811 several ships took out over 10,600 skins. By the time Richard Henry Dana came to San Francisco in 1835, the sea otter business was virtually finished, although Dana was intrigued by other wildlife such as the herds of tule elk that he watched from his ship off the Marin coast: 'Herds of hundreds and hundreds of red deer and the stag with his high branching antlers were bounding about looking at us for the moment and then starting off affrighted of the noises that we made for purpose of seeing the variety of their beautiful attitudes and motions.'"

The last California grizzly bear to be killed was found in Tulare County in 1922. Another grizzly, possibly its mate, was seen several times in Sequoia National Park in 1924; no one knows what happened to it. No other grizzlies have been seen in California's wild country. The sea otter was to come close to extinction in California. One small

Island wildlife has historically proven to be dangerously susceptible to extirpation. The Channel Islands populations of bald eagles, ospreys, and peregrine falcons all became extinct. Recently, however, the bald eagle has been successfully reintroduced on Santa Catalina Island. Overhunted to the point of extinction in the nineteenth century, the northern fur seal returned unassisted to San Miguel Island in the early 1960s.

Northern Fur Seals, San Miguel Island, California

band survived off the Monterey coast, and the current California population has descended from it. Tule elk were also reduced to a small remnant group protected by the Miller and Lux ranch in Kern County, but they are now being brought back slowly to many areas of coastal California. Many other species have gone, but for others the settlement of California, at least in its early stages, brought on a period of abundance. Starker Leopold wrote a definitive book on one of these species, *The California Quail*.

"The peak of the California quail population, occurring in the period 1860 to 1895, would correspond very well to 'the era of settlement and crude agriculture,' which in California should also include 'the era of crude pastoralism.' The initial widespread ecologic impact on the landscape of California was triggered by the development of immense herds of livestock. . . . Concurrently, the better soils were being broken by the plow and planted to grains, hay, orchards, and vineyards. The first major cash crop was barley, but by 1860 wheat had become dominant, with a yield of nearly 6,000,000 bushels. Grapes and fruit trees were added with the advent of irrigation systems.

"Picture the landscape in a typical valley of the inner coastal ranges of central California about 1870. The oaks and sycamores along the stream course, tangled with wild grape vines and undergrown with shrubs, had not yet been disturbed. But the rich alluvium on benches bordering the stream was plowed in small patches, and the more accessible level areas were planted to grain.

"A few small orchards and vineyards had been set out in areas easily irrigated from the stream. The grassy hills were being heavily grazed, breaking up the native bunchgrasses and allowing an intrusion of many seedbearing Mediterranean forbs such as filaree and clovers. These same forbs densely invaded the poorly kept orchards and vineyards and likewise sprinkled the grain stands. One could scarcely envision a better habitat for quail. Food, cover, and water, occurring in abundance on soils not yet depleted of their virgin fertility, would stimulate production of a great flush of seed-eating birds, such as quail. Some such ecologic circumstance unquestionably underlay the abundance of quail in the early years of settlement.

Looking down at the southern reaches of San Francisco Bay from high up in the Diablo Range to the east, one can see the mountains and valleys of the central Coast Range disappear into the waters of the bay. The depression formed by San Francisco Bay separates the central Coast Range from the northern Coast Range, creating a physical barrier that has a profound influence on the dispersal and speciation of plants and animals on both sides of the channel.

Central Coast Range, South San Francisco Bay, California

"A point that needs great emphasis is that the fortuitous production of optimum vegetation for quail took place on soils brimming with the stored fertility and organic matter of the ages. . . . It is unrealistic to believe that these pioneer conditions could be fully restored today by proper land management. Overgrazing, overcropping, and surface erosion have stripped most lands of that accumulated richness that came with centuries of soil maturation under native vegetation. Perhaps only the deep alluvial valleys have retained the basic capacity to fully renew their original productivity, and those are the areas now cultivated most intensively and mechanically. We must take the sensible view that the great quail peak of the late 1800s is a glamorous relic of the past—a relic we wish fully to understand but that we can never actually reproduce.

"By the same token, a virgin forest initially logged may produce a rich second-growth of brush and tree reproduction that in turn may support a fabulous deer population. No subsequent cutting of second-growth timber produces quite the same profusion of animal life. A newly filled reservoir often supports a tremendous fishery, but as the organic matter and available nutrients of the bottom are drawn away, productivity of the basic food chains slows down and the fishery dwindles" (1977a, pp. 33–34).

Although quail reached their peak numbers in the late 1800s, it was not until the 1950s that California's deer population reached its greatest abundance. Three races of deer occurred in Spanish California—the southern mule deer from the Los Angeles area south into Baja California, the California mule deer north from there into Monterey and San Benito counties, and the Columbian black-tailed deer farther north extending up the coast to Alaska. In fact, there are not many obvious differences between these races. From all evidence they were reasonably abundant, even numerous in some places, in Spanish times, although not in the large populations they were later to attain. Following settlement, deer numbers declined as they were hunted for subsistence and subsequently for the market. However, with protection from hunting and with the removal of predators, deer populations started to

Before the winter rains create extensive inland wetland habitats, virtually all of the canvasback ducks wintering in California may be found on the open waters of San Francisco and San Pablo bays. Here the canvasbacks gather in tremendous flocks called "rafts," looking more like a flotilla of ships.

Canvasback Ducks, San Francisco Bay, California

increase. Some account of this was revealed by the extensive deer studies that Starker Leopold started work on in 1948 and continued to supervise during most of his working career:

"Ralph S. Roy, who had spent all of his sixty-eight years on a 2,000-acre dairy ranch near Lagunitas, Marin County, was fourteen years old (1894) when he saw his first deer and it was several years before he saw another. As he grew to maturity, however, deer became increasingly common, and by 1920 several legal bucks were killed each year on the ranch. In 1947 members of the family and their friends killed thirty bucks on the same area, and Mr. Roy was in our office to report acute deer damage to his crops and orchards. . . .

"Game Warden Orbin Philbrick states that between 1895 and 1905 he saw only two deer in the Adelaida area near Paso Robles, San Luis Obispo County. Now he sees up to two hundred in a day in the same area (1950). . . . It would appear that by 1940 the better deer ranges in California were fully stocked, and in many cases overstocked" (1952, p. 21).

The increase of deer in the coastal region is related in part to what has happened to the extensive areas of chaparral. As Leopold explained, "Chaparral is one of the extensive vegetational formations of the coastal ranges of California. . . . There are, in fact, many distinctive local types of chaparral, made up of quite different species of shrubs. Along the humid coast, some of the dominant shrub genera are coyote bush (*Baccharis*), wild lilac *(Ceanothus)*, poison oak *(Rhus)*, and various oaks *(Quercus)*. In more arid situations these genera may be replaced by chamise (*Adenostoma*), manzanita (*Arctostaphylos*), or sage (*Artemisia*). All types of chaparral are similar, however, in having a dense, closed canopy with sparse herbaceous ground cover.

"Chaparral often occurs on steep slopes or on gravel outwash fans where the raw, inorganic soils are too weak to sustain woodland or grassland communities. On these unstable soils, California's Mediterranean climate, with its long, dry, almost rainless summers, has stimulated the evolution of chaparral as the most appropriate type of protective plant cover. The scrub oak, a typical plant of the chaparral, was known to the Spanish settlers as *chaparro*, and from this term 'chaparral' has come to represent dense shrubland growth.

The drainage systems of our major rivers flow toward the coast, where they empty into the Pacific Ocean. Estuaries formed there by these rivers and numerous small creeks, freshwater ponds, and lagoons comprise the precious coastal wetland habitat. The Tijuana Slough and River Estuary, one of the least altered coastal wetland habitats in southern California, provides significant wintering areas and migration stopovers for waterfowl, shorebirds, waders, gulls, and terns.

Heermann's Gull and Elegant Terns, Tijuana River Estuary, California

"California's dry summers are also favorable for fires, which over the centuries have periodically swept over the state's brushlands, causing all chaparral species to become adapted to fire in one way or another. Destruction of chaparral by fire is normally followed by slow recovery, which works differently in the different species. Some chaparral shrubs crown-sprout after burning, whereas others regenerate by seeding" (1977a, pp. 56–57).

"Prior to settlement, deer seem to have occurred principally along 'edges' where forest and grassland met or on recent burns in the forest. . . . In central and western California, chaparral is spreading into grassland and oak-woodland, due largely, I feel quite certain, to past overgrazing. . . . In any event, the extension of chaparral, at least aided and abetted by grazing, is creating deer range where there was none before . . . deer seem to achieve maximum densities in areas of disturbed vegetation which produce palatable shrubs or tree reproduction as secondary stages in plant succession. Logging, fire, and grazing are the three principal influences which in the past have created, or at least improved, most of our present deer ranges. In excess, of course, the same influences can destroy deer range.

"The first tenet of deer management in my way of thinking is deliberate manipulation of plant successions to maintain the high carrying capacities of our ranges. . . .

"Controlled burning is the cheapest tool where applicable. The controlled use of fire has been established practice for years in managing . . . game and livestock range in northern California. Current studies in California seem to show that judicious, rotational burning may be both safe and effective in improving certain chaparral ranges for deer. In short, the fact that fire can be enormously destructive when out of control should not preclude its regulated use in deer management where other forest values are not endangered.

"Moderate browsing of shrubs and tree reproduction induces sprouting, thereby increasing the volume of available forage and actually raising the carrying capacity of a range. The palatability of sprouts is higher than that of unbrowsed twigs, and . . . the nutritive value may be somewhat higher. Likewise, the sprouts are within reach of the deer. Their regular pruning prevents the plant from growing out of

The Audubon's cottontail rabbit, stretching in front of its rocky home, is active in the early morning or late afternoon and is never far from some form of cover. It frequently eats fallen fruit and leaves and in turn is preyed upon by snakes, hawks, owls, coyotes, foxes, and bobcats. The rabbit's senses of hearing and sight are highly developed, hence its large ears and eyes.

Audubon's Cottontail, Carrizo Plain, California

reach of the deer and assures another crop of forage for the next year. In this manner deer can improve their own range up to a certain point.

"But when excess numbers of deer occupy a range, they exhaust the vigor of the forage plants by overbrowsing, with consequent reduction in range productivity. The plants may die completely or in the case of taller species simply cease sprouting below the browse line.

"When the volume of forage falls below the requirements of the herd, or when the food is rendered temporarily unavailable by deep snow, mortality ensues—sometimes wholesale starvation, at other times gradual decrease following lowered reproductive success. In warmer climates (such as coastal California) actual decimation often results from parasitism or disease, but the underlying cause is still inadequate nutrition" (1950, pp. 572–576).

Leopold's deer studies enabled him to account for the amazing abundance of deer in California during the period from the late 1940s until the 1960s, the result of the logging, burning of chaparral, and grazing practices of earlier decades. These studies also indicated the need both to control deer numbers through hunting, and thus prevent the overuse and destruction of their habitat, and to manipulate vegetation through controlled burning, managed tree cutting, and regulated grazing to create and maintain adequate deer habitat. Despite Leopold's efforts, however, deer numbers were not controlled, nor was there to be any large-scale program for deer range improvement. In the 1960s, as he had predicted, deer numbers began to decline. They are now, in the 1980s, well below earlier levels.

The abundance of deer in Spanish California resulted in an abundance of their chief predator, the mountain lion. The Santa Lucia Mountains and the Diablo Range of the central Coast Ranges have long been centers for mountain lion survival, even during the years when these big cats were persistently hunted, trapped, and otherwise persecuted. Leopold has written of his encounters with mountain lions in a wilderness area of Mexico:

"I never really expected to see a mountain lion. The big, mysterious cats are almost entirely nocturnal in habit, and it is rare indeed that one is observed on the move in daylight hours. One foggy morning I slipped quietly over a low rise in the pine forest and two hundred yards

The six largest of southern California's eight Channel Islands support populations of island foxes. A diminutive relative of the gray fox found on the mainland, these island foxes live out their lives hunting for rodents and foraging for fruits. As is the case with most insular endemic wildlife, their existence is precarious.

Island Foxes, Santa Cruz Island, California

ahead on a rocky slope were *three lions* stalking majestically between the boulders. One animal led, and the other two followed forty yards behind. There was little visible difference in size, but I presumed the leader was a lioness and the others were her grown young of 1947. They were through hunting apparently, for they loafed along, pausing now and then to preen their coats. When the leader stopped, the other two held up likewise and kept their distance. I finally shot (without scoring a kill) and sent them all bounding over the boulders. . . .

"On another occasion [Robert] McCabe and I were hunting turkeys on a steep canyon face near camp when there commenced on the far side of the canyon a powerful roaring, reminiscent of an African lion but of higher pitch and shorter duration. This stirring serenade continued off and on for nearly half an hour. McCabe, who was below me on the slope, could see the author of the disturbance was a large mountain lion (he guessed a male) parading along the rocky ledges and roaring occasionally as he walked. The observation is of considerable interest, since there has been a longstanding controversy among naturalists as to whether mountain lions roar at all. There are some who have hunted lions for years and killed dozens or even hundreds without hearing one give any vocal expression other than a snarl or hiss" (1949, pp. 9–10).

Raymond F. Dasmann
June 1984

The mountain lion stealthily prowls throughout the central Coast Range, hunting primarily for deer. Through removing the very old, sick, or infirm individuals, lions can help to keep deer herds healthy.

Mountain Lion, Diablo Range, California

California Condor, Transverse Range, California (Photograph by Tupper Ansel Blake, Courtesy of U.S. Fish and Wildlife Service)

A creature of undeniable majesty, the California condor is the largest bird in North America, boasting a wingspan of up to nine and a half feet. To see this condor sweep in controlled flight over chaparral-covered slopes and ridge crests is a rare and awe-inspiring experience. The white patch on the underside of its wing distinguishes it from the much smaller common turkey vulture.

California Condor Young, Transverse Range, California (Photograph by Tupper Ansel Blake, Courtesy of U.S. Fish and Wildlife Service)

Reduced to a remnant population, the California condor has its stronghold in the state's central and southern mountains. Each year fewer and fewer chicks are born in the wild. Those that are begin life in a cliffside cave.

Band-Tailed Pigeons, Santa Lucia Range, California

After breeding in the more northerly latitudes of British Columbia, Washington, and Oregon, band-tailed pigeons head for California, their principal wintering area, with its mild climate and many oak trees, where they scour the hills and valleys of the entire central Coast Range in pursuit of acorns.

Limantour Spit, Point Reyes, California

Coastal wetlands vary tremendously in the features they offer and the kinds of wildlife habitats they support. Some have sandy beaches along the barrier bars that separate lagoons from the open ocean. Others have deep channels and basins that are never drained completely, even during the lowest of tides. Major habitat types within coastal wetlands are estuaries, freshwater lagoons, freshwater marshes, tidal salt marshes, sloughs, tidal mudflats, river channels, and open water. Coastal wetlands provide significant wintering areas and migrational stopovers for Pacific flyway waterfowl, shorebirds, and wading birds.

Salt Marsh Harvest Mouse, San Francisco Bay, California

104

The salt marsh harvest mouse has adapted to a high salt content in its diet, but in most cases it cannot survive with sea water as its sole source of fluid; winter rains and summer fogs provide necessary freshwater supplement. The mouse here is shown amid picklewood, a plant that provides it with food and cover. When the terrain is too low and wet for picklewood to grow successfully, the salt marsh becomes dominated by coarse and hardy cord grass, which creates a dark green bank along the bay's edge.

California Clapper Rail, San Francisco Bay, California

The California clapper rail is a bird found
almost exclusively in the salt marshes of
San Francisco Bay. At low tide, these rails
work along the edges of marshes and on the
banks of sloughs, eating worms, crabs, and
other small animals in the soft mud.

Lesser Sandhill Cranes, Carrizo Plain, California

Leaving the great treeless tundras of northern North America, lesser sandhill cranes
move south across Canada and the western
United States, wintering in great numbers
in California. Their well-known rolling
cry as they pass to and fro in migration is
a sound of the wild that, once heard, is
never forgotten. In migration they fly very
high, in lines somewhat like those of ducks
and geese. Their legs and necks are held
stretched out to full extent. Because of
their extreme shyness and their habit of
foraging far out on open plains, they find
the isolated Soda Lake and the Carrizo
Plain, where some seven to ten thousand
lesser sandhill cranes winter, to their
liking.

California Sea Lions, San Miguel Island, California

Basking on the warm sands of San Miguel
Island, a herd of female and young California sea lions remains under the watchful
eye of the herdmaster, an old bull. At the
slightest intrusion toward them by another
adult male, the bull will roar so loudly as
to drown the noise of the heaviest surf.
Combat will take place if the warning goes
unheeded.

Little Sur River, Big Sur Coast, California

108

The Santa Lucia Range is one of the most prominent sections of the extensive Coast Range system, dominating the coast of California for more than a hundred miles from San Luis Obispo to Point Pinos, south of Monterey Bay. The rugged slopes of the mountains are a sheer drop to the surf-washed rocks, which are clothed in tangles of kelp forest and dotted with basking sea lions. The steep cliffline is broken at points along the coast where streams such as the Little Sur River enter the sea. These rivers and creeks bring wildlife diversity to the area, affording freshwater riparian habitat shaded by willows and alders.

Steller Sea Lions, Farallon Islands, California

A male Steller sea lion can be up to ten to twelve feet long and may weigh a ton or even more, while his mates are less than half as big and more slender. For a sea-going flesh eater with a broad neck, a light brown hide, and lion-shaped eyes, the northern species' original name of leo ma-rinus, or "lion of the sea," seemed appropriate to G. W. Steller, the naturalist who named it. An island shore, such as on the Farallones, is its hereditary breeding ground and nursery.

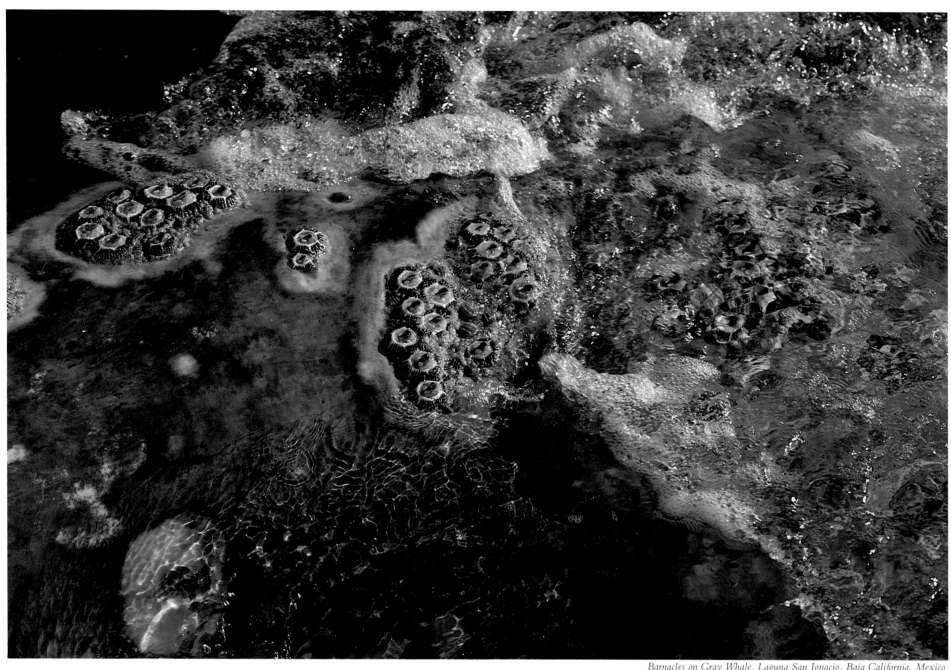

Barnacles on Gray Whale, Laguna San Ignacio, Baja California, Mexico

The gray whale makes a yearly trek between Alaska and Mexico, and in so doing passes along the California coast twice, a migration as predictable as those of swans and geese. A species of barnacle goes along for the ride. These barnacles may occur in small groups almost anywhere on the whale's body or on the surfaces of the flukes and flippers, but they are most abundant on areas exposed to the air when the whale surfaces. The dorsal, or upper, portion of the whale is most often exposed, of course, and these areas are also those most directly exposed to food-carrying water currents as the whale stirs up sediments from the ocean bed.

Northern Elephant Seals, Farallon Islands, California

After years of low numbers, northern elephant seal populations recently sky-rocketed. A pair of young elephant seals throw back their heads to call, making their presence in the colony known to one and all. Their large, dark eyes are precision instruments, providing them with the excellent vision so important for under-water hunting. The folds along their backs encase a layer of fat that is several inches thick, insulating them against injury by other elephant seals and the cold ocean waters.

The Great Arch, Farallon Islands, California

Some seabirds, such as cormorants, pelicans, and most gulls, spend most of their time near the shore, but others come to land only during the breeding season (petrels, puffins, and auklets, for example). All seabirds gather in colonies during the breeding season—on islands, offshore rocks, and mainland cliffs. Two California regions, the Farallon Islands and the north coast from Cape Mendocino to the Oregon border, contain the largest number of breeding seabirds. The sites of these colonies are the most important habitat for seabirds because reproduction, and therefore continuation of the species, depends on continued and safe access to these areas.

Marbled Godwits, Point Piedras Blancas, California

The sand beaches of California are favorite wintering and feeding grounds of marbled godwits. These long-billed birds pick up small molluscs and swallow them with tremendous dexterity. The same skill also allows them to eat snails, crustaceans, and insects. A beach walk becomes more memorable when shared with a colorful and stately group of marbled godwits.

Shorebirds, Limantour Estero, Point Reyes, California

Shorebirds of more than a score of species swarm the California marshes and mud-flats in spring on their way to northern breeding grounds, returning again in late summer when they make their way back south. Some shorebirds travel almost the length of two continents between their summer and winter homes. These long-distance travelers economize on their time and energy by feeding when the tides are low and migrating when the tides are high, regardless of whether it is day or night.

Western Gulls, Farallon Islands, California

Before the encroachments of civilization gave the western gull an easy way of earning its living as a scavenger, its main food source was the sea, where it preyed on schools of small fish. The western gull is the most noticeable and abundant seabird along the California coast. One wonders how the western gulls' immaculate, snow-white plumage is kept so spotlessly clean, given the untidy feeding habits of these birds.

Snowy Plover, Limantour Estero, Point Reyes, California

The only shorebird to nest along the sandy beaches of California is the snowy plover. Completely exposed, both bird and eggs depend on intricate color patterns to break up their image and avoid detection.

Western Gulls and Brandt's Cormorants, Farallon Islands, California

On its breeding grounds, the most important food supply of the western gull consists
of the eggs and young of other birds, near
which it almost always nests. Riding the
wind, a group of western gulls glides over
a colony of Brandt's cormorants, looking
for that opportunity.

Tufted Puffin, Farallon Islands, California

The tufted puffin, called a "sea parrot" by whalers of old, has a beautiful bill contrived of eighteen plates, sixteen of which are deciduous—they fall away at the end of breeding season. Spending its life at sea, the bird comes to land only to nest and to raise its young.

Rock Crab, Farallon Islands, California

The rock crab is a common inhabitant of the high intertidal zone. Ed Ricketts, the gifted marine biologist and cohort of John Steinbeck, referred to this important scavenger as "the pugnacious little rock crab, without which any rocky beach must seem lonesome and quiet."

Douglas-Fir Forest, Inverness Ridge, Point Reyes, California

7 :: THE NORTH WOODS

The northern Coast Range of California displays a dense cloak of evergreen forest over rugged mountainsides. This is the southern portion of the greatest and most diverse stand of conifers, or cone-bearing trees, in the world, the Douglas-fir forest; stands of these tall, picturesque trees are nearly pure in many places. These forests and mountains are prime habitat for some of California's larger and rarer wildlife: the black bear, mountain lion, river otter, fisher, and wolverine, as well as bald eagles and peregrine falcons.

The northwest of California differs in many ways from the rest of the state, and its affinities, both ecological and cultural, lie northward with the forested region of Oregon and Washington. This is land where the lumber industry holds sway in forests of redwood and Douglas fir, Sitka spruce and red cedar. Unlike the Sierra, where timbered areas are mostly in national forests, the redwood country is largely held in private ownership. Efforts to establish effective protection, as in the Redwood National Park, have had to overcome the political power and financial influence of the timber industries.

Deep forests and complex mountain systems characterize the north coast. Although the mountains do not equal the height of the Sierra, they are steep, rugged, and reach a respectable 9,000 feet in the Trinity Alps. Some of the state's largest rivers, the Klamath, Trinity, Mad, and Eel, drain this region. Redwood forests are confined to the coastal plains and mountains, except where they reach inland along river valleys. Wherever they grow, you will find summer fogs and usually heavy winter rains. Periodically, excessive rains swell the rivers to almost unbelievable depths, and flood waters, carrying redwood logs as battering rams, sweep the river basins free of man-made structures.

The north coast is still one of the wildest regions of California. It is a stronghold for black bears and mountain lions, a home for the Roosevelt elk and for fishers, mink, and river otters. This is the land of Steller's jays, ruffed grouse, varied thrush, mountain beavers, trilliums, rhododendrons, huckleberries, and salal. Pileated woodpeckers and spotted owls haunt the old forests. The streams once swarmed with king and silver salmon, steelhead and cutthroat trout. Despite the dams and water diversions, fisherfolk still come to the northern rivers with high hope and are often rewarded for their skill.

121

The future of wildlife in this area is tied, as nowhere else in California, to the behavior of foresters and the timber industry. It was this influence that concerned Starker Leopold:

"The social values of wildlife and the desirability of retaining our heritage of native animals are recognized in a myriad of laws, both state and federal, that protect all but a few pest species from wanton destruction. The animals themselves receive adequate protection from the law; not so the habitat in which they live. It is illegal to kill a woodpecker but perfectly legal to cut down the dead tree harboring its nest, which in the end of course eliminates the woodpecker permanently.

"Forestland, public and private, provides indispensable habitat for much of our surviving wildlife. An increasing share of this forestland is today coming under intensive, high-yield management. The assertion is often made that managed forests constitute a haven for wild creatures. My own observation does not bear out this generalization. The overriding purpose of intensive forest management is to raise the yield of forest products; the incidental effects on animal life may vary from beneficial to catastrophic, depending on the species and its ecologic requirements" (1978a, p. 108).

"Forest management practices affect the diversity and abundance of wild animals by altering the successional stages of the forest. Some of the native American birds and mammals that evolved to fit the wide spectrum of niches the continent offers prefer or require a rather specialized habitat. Some species live only in tall mature forests. Others thrive in forest openings or in early brushland stages of forest regeneration. The point is evident that to maintain the full spectrum of native vertebrates, it is necessary to preserve or create areas representing all stages of forest succession, particularly the mature forest. Intensive forest practice tends to shorten rotations and to truncate succession, reducing or eliminating animals adapted to live in mature stands" (1978a, p. 109).

"Perhaps the most widespread forest practice—and one of least benefit to wildlife—is the culture of conifers in pure, even-aged stands. In many situations, such stands are the highest yielding form of forest management. . . . Among the most intensively managed forest areas in the country is the Douglas-fir zone . . . where a great deal of forest

Rivers such as the Klamath are rich and diverse resources—ribbons of life. They are used by fourteen species of anadromous fish, which move between the ocean and freshwater streams. Four species chiefly inhabit the river estuaries, and about forty-five species are confined exclusively to the rivers. In addition, numerous birds, mammals, insects, and plants depend on the river systems.

Klamath River, California

123

land is devoted to the culture of fast-growing, even-aged stands of Douglas fir. The redwood region of northern California is maintained in dense, fully stocked stands with little attractiveness to wildlife" (1978a, pp. 110–111).

"These monocultures are virtually devoid of wildlife after the canopy closes. Shrub undergrowth is shaded out, or its elimination is hastened with herbicide spraying. Snags and mature trees are removed with the first cutting and are not allowed to regenerate. Hole-nesting birds and mammals are eliminated for lack of shelter, and most other kinds of wildlife find little or no food. I have driven through such plantations in northern California where a bluejay would have to pack a lunch to get across" (1978b, p. 9).

"The effort to bring suitable sites into 'tree farm' production for conifer timber still has a long way to go. It is not the present status of the process that concerns me but rather the trend. As even-age planting progresses, the carrying capacity of the land for wildlife will decrease progressively. Species dependent upon mature forest will inevitably disappear; the process will produce the 'rare and endangered species' of tomorrow. The spotted owl . . . appears to live only in mature conifer stands. When the last of these are logged, the spotted owl will be a rare bird indeed.

"There are acknowledged wildlife benefits from clearcutting to weigh against the losses among species of the mature mixed-age forest. During early successional stages of forest regeneration, shrubs and forbs characteristically invade cleared land, as they did the slashed-and-burned lands of past years. Besides deer, some granivorous birds and various small mammals also respond favorably to the forb-shrub stage of succession. The balance is not entirely negative.

"But in contrast to the clearcut, even-aged trend in silvicultural practice, selective logging of individual mature trees has far less adverse impact on wildlife. A selectively cut forest is actually a mosaic of large and small trees, openings, and thickets and sometimes includes a mixture of hardwoods and conifers. . . . It is relatively easy to adjust a selective cut to provide varied wildlife habitat while at the same time yielding a reasonable crop of logs. . . .

The Columbian black-tailed deer occupies several types of habitat, from coniferous forest to grassland with shrubs. In all cases, browse plants are necessary for survival. The fall is rutting season. With antlers at the ready, males seek battle with other bucks to establish dominance and breed with females. In spring and early summer, the young are born. These fawns, usually a pair, are able to walk a few minutes after birth. Spotted coats in these early months help conceal the young from predators.

Columbian Black-Tailed Deer, Scott Mountains, California

"A fully developed climax forest is called 'decadent' in the parlance of production forestry, and old growth stands are decreasing steadily in acreage. Yet as we have seen, some birds and mammals are obligatory residents of such decadent forests.

"A classic example of a climax forest bird was the ivory-billed woodpecker. Apparently dependent on the presence of mature southern hardwoods, the ivory-bill disappeared to the point of extinction when these trees were cut in logging or for agricultural clearing. . . .

"Many other climax bird species have decreased in range and abundance as the virgin forests have shrunk. In western conifer forests, the widespread pileated woodpecker is now declining, as are a number of insectivorous forest birds, including various parids, flycatchers, thrushes, warblers, and woodpeckers" (1978a, pp. 113–114).

"If forest managers are willing, there are many ways in which timber practice can be modified on the ground to provide wildlife habitat, with moderate—but not excessive—sacrifice in board-feet production and economic yield. The problem is not beyond solution biologically, but it requires compromise, one component of which is reduced profit. . . . The management procedures that enhance wildlife habitat are nearly all of a sort that cut profits to the timber operator: leaving snags and potential snags in the forest, leaving strips or corners of mature trees uncut, keeping clearcut blocks small, desisting from excessive use of herbicides and pesticides, maintaining some uneven-aged stands when even-aged stands are simpler to manage mechanically. On public forests these silvicultural adjustments are possible and fully justified" (1978a, p. 118).

Of course, the north coast of California is not all forested, but it includes a wide range of vegetation types. Grassland, chaparral, and oak woodland once provided a home for an abundance of grizzly bears, which have since been replaced to some extent by the black bear. The rangelands of the north coast are highly productive and have supported a thriving cattle and sheep population, which has in turn caused conflict with the larger predatory animals—coyotes, bears, bobcats, mountain lions. Leopold's views on predatory animal control have had a strong influence on government policy toward predators and are worth repeating here:

King salmon are anadromous fish—that is, they grow and mature in the ocean and then swim into fresh water to reproduce and die. Along the coast of northern California, these fish enter the Klamath, Smith, and Eel river systems, returning to the streams in which they were born.

King Salmon, Klamath River, California

"In a frontier community, animal life is cheap and held in low esteem. Thus it was that a frontiersman would shoot a bison for its tongue or an eagle for amusement. In America we inherited a particularly prejudiced and unsympathetic view of animals that may at times be dangerous or troublesome. From the days of the mountain men through the period of conquest and settlement of the West, incessant war was waged against the wolf, grizzly, cougar, and the lowly coyote, and even today in the remaining backwoods the maxim persists that the only good varmint is a dead one.

"But times and social values change. As our culture becomes more sophisticated and more urbanized, wild animals begin to assume recreational significance at which the pioneer would have scoffed. Americans by the millions swarm out of the cities on vacation seeking a refreshing taste of the wilderness, of which animal life is the living manifestation. Some come to hunt; others to look, or to photograph. Recognition of this reappraisal of animal value is manifest in the myriad restrictive laws and regulations that now protect nearly all kinds of animals from capricious destruction.

"Only some of the predators and troublesome rodents and birds remain unprotected by law or public conscience. In many localities bounties are paid for their scalps, and government hunters are employed for their control. In point of fact, there are numerous situations where control of predators, rodents, and even some birds is essential to protect important agricultural and pastoral interests or human health and safety. The problem is to differentiate these local situations where control is justified from the numerous cases where the same species of animals have social values far in excess of the negligible damage they cause. The large carnivores in particular are objects of fascination to most Americans, and for every person whose sheep may be molested by a coyote there are perhaps a thousand others who would thrill to hear a coyote chorus in the night" (1969).

Shown in their bulky nest of sticks, three young ospreys watch the arrival of an adult. Having been confined to their nest since birth, these birds are almost ready to fledge and await the day when they will fly and hunt along rivers and lakes, diving for fish.

Osprey, Inverness Ridge, Point Reyes, California

However, the ranchers who herd their pickup trucks around the back roads of Humboldt and Mendocino counties have not read Leopold's words and would not be impressed if they did. Although the predatory-animal control policies of the government were changed for a number of years through Leopold's efforts, and those of his co-workers, the pendulum has swung back the other way. Those coyotes that survive in the north coast mountains must learn to avoid sheep and not to join in any night-time chorus with their friends.

Starker Leopold did not spend much time in the north woods. The duck marshes of the Central Valley, the Sierra, the Great Basin, and the quail country of the southern Coast Ranges were more his habitat. But all the creatures that live in the deep woods owe him a debt for his efforts on their behalf.

Raymond F. Dasmann
June 1984

A line of common mergansers drifting downriver is a beautiful sight. Often called the "fish duck" or "sawbill" because its bill is edged with sharp, horny "teeth" and a hooked tip, the common merganser is an excellent swimmer and diver and can remain under water for as much as one or two minutes in pursuit of its prey.

Common Mergansers, Redwood Creek, California

California Quail, Inverness Ridge, Point Reyes, California

132

"*Of all the birds native to the state of California, none is more universally enjoyed and appreciated than the California Quail. The handsome plumage, pert demeanor, and melodious calls are appealing to everyone fortunate enough to know the species, and it is not surprising that in 1931 the State Legislature by unanimous acclamation declared the California Quail to be the State Bird of California.*"

A. Starker Leopold
The California Quail

Robin, Prairie Creek, California

The tremendous forests of the northern Coast Range owe their existence, in part, to the fact that the region is one of drizzling, misty rains, notable for long duration rather than intensity. The wildlife has adapted to this climate, and birds such as the robin go about their business rain or shine.

Storm Clouds, Diablo Range, California

8 :: CALIFORNIA FAREWELL

Starker Leopold left no farewell message that would provide a fitting conclusion to this book. If he had, I think it might have read like his "Adios, Gavilan," which he wrote in an earlier time about another country, the Gavilan River region of Mexico. What he had to say was this:

"Summer waned and the hour of departure arrived. On August 25, when the last recalcitrant mule was packed, we turned our horses up the familiar trail to 'top out' for the final time. What can we expect to find when next we return? Will there still be wolves to howl at dusk? Will young pines have filled the places of the fallen patriarchs? Will even higher floods scour the river course? I fear to hazard a guess. Certain it is, however, that the wilderness will be gone. Ubiquitous man has claimed even the Gavilan.

"Though I lament the passing of the wilderness, I mean to pick no quarrel with civilization as a whole; automobiles, modern houses, and beefsteaks are as much appreciated by me as by anyone else. I question merely its universal spread. The Gavilan can offer little to the 'good life.' It will produce some beef and some lumber and then probably be left stripped and gutted to its basaltic core. Might it not have yielded more the way it was? Must there be a cow on *every* hill, a road in *every* valley?

"In the United States we are making some progress toward preserving examples of primitive America. The National Park Service and the U.S. Forest Service have set aside some magnificent areas for preservation in the natural state. These and other remnants of unspoiled country are being stoutly defended by a little band of patriots, poor in purse but rich in spirit, who have joined to form a Wilderness Society. But in Mexico, the wilderness is still on its own.

"I would like to think that there is another river filtering off hillsides of golden grama and winding under virgin pine. May my son some day explore its rimrocks and imagine there are still Apaches in its tributaries" (1949, p. 13).

"The only possible force that could be motivating the efforts to preserve natural areas is the moral conviction that it is right—that we owe it to ourselves and to the good earth that supports us to curb our avarice to the extent of leaving a few spots untouched and unexploited" (Leopold, quoted by Margaret E. Murie in "Alaska Journey," *Living Wilderness*, Spring 1984, p. 44).

Starker Leopold's words about a cow on every hill and a road in every valley impressed me. During seven years in Switzerland, I spent much time climbing ridges and mountains trying to find some real "back country" where the presence of people had not left its impression on the land. But there seemed to be always, regardless of what the maps indicated, a cow on every hill and a road in every valley. The Swiss did not seem to mind. They, perhaps, had no memory, as I had, of country that was really wild. For a small country they have done well. There is a national park and there are many nature reserves. But there is no *real* wildness, let alone wilderness. People are everywhere. To those who know no better this may not seem to matter. The bears, the lynxes, the wolves are gone—but so what? Nobody remembers. I remember, although I am not a citizen. I have seen foxes and roe deer, chamois and ibex, and I have flushed capercaillie from their roosts in spruce trees—but this was not enough.

There is a wildness in California still that is in the blood of those who grew up here. It does not exist only within those areas designated as wilderness or national parks, but also in the "back blocks"—the hinterland of lands that are otherwise used for other purposes. There is a feeling that back beyond the next ridge there is still wild country. And even beyond that there is an invasion of the wild into the tame that for some of us brings a feeling of security. I have seen a mountain lion on the campus at the university in Santa Cruz. I have seen many deer and coyotes and a number of skunks, raccoons, possums, weasels, and golden eagles in the same area. A bobcat has wandered through my back yard. I have listed sixty species of birds seen from or in that same back garden area—and it is not extensive. But there is still here, next to the more than four and a half million people of the San Francisco Bay area, country that is essentially wild. A few species are missing, but most of those that the Indians knew are still here. Admittedly they are depleted in numbers, but they still have viable populations. With a little effort, and a small sacrifice of commercial gain, they could be brought back. We still have a chance to save wild California.

There are those who say we have done enough. Half of the state is protected to some degree by the National Park Service, the Forest Service, the Bureau of Land Management, the military, and so on. But the degree of protection must be carefully examined and monitored, or you will notice that your favorite grove has been logged, and the most exquisite landscape is now being strip-mined. There are many natural areas and habitats of many rare and endangered species that have little protection. The streamside woodland, the fresh and salt water marshes, the forests of rare pines or cypresses, the habitats of endangered plant species—all have inadequate protection. Most of our existing protected areas are inadequate in either size or shape to accomplish the objectives of protection they were intended to provide. Above and beyond that is the question of total land management. Can we manage our commercial farms, pastures, rangelands, and forests in such a way that they can continue to provide for our human needs on into the future? Perhaps if we can really meet our own needs on a *sustainable* basis, we will also meet the needs of other species, our companions in the biosphere, our hope for the future of the human habitat. Meanwhile, as we work toward that goal, we had better set aside and protect every piece of wild California that we can remove from the path of devastation and mindless change. It is the least we can do.

Raymond F. Dasmann
June 1984

Bishop Pines, Point Reyes, California

The Bishop pine is found only in a few isolated locations near the California coast. These are the last remaining descendants of forebears that once occupied larger territories during a more favorable geological era. Often referred to as a fire pine or closed-cone pine, the Bishop pine has cones that cannot release their seeds unless fire melts the resinous coating that glues the scales together. To come upon a bluff-top grove of Bishop pine gives one the feeling of viewing a scene from a Japanese woodcut print.

137

Salt Marsh, South San Francisco Bay, California

Many species of wildlife can and do live in a variety of habitats, but there are other life forms that are restricted to a single habitat because they lack the ability to adapt to any other. The salt marshes of San Francisco Bay, with their high content of salt in both water and soil, nurture many extremely specialized organisms.

Farallon Islands, California

"There are some who can live without
wild things, and some who cannot. . . .
  "Like winds and sunsets, wild things
were taken for granted until progress began
to do away with them. Now we face the
question whether a still higher 'standard of
living' is worth its cost in things natural,
wild, and free. For us of the minority, the
opportunity to see geese is more important
than television, and the chance to find a
pasque-flower is a right as inalienable as
free speech."

Aldo Leopold
A Sand County Almanac

1949.   "Adios, Gavilan." *Pacific Discovery* 2, no. 1:4–13.

1950.   "Deer in Relation to Plant Succession." *Transactions, Fifteenth North American Wildlife Conference*, Washington, D.C., pp. 571–580.

1952.   "A Survey of California Deer Herds, Their Ranges and Management Problems." Game Bulletin 6. California Department of Fish and Game, Sacramento. With W. M. Longhurst and R. F. Dasmann.

1953.   "Too Many Deer." *Sierra Club Bulletin* 38, no. 8:51–57.

1956.   "Hunting for the Masses—Can Game Departments Supply It?" Thirty-sixth Annual Conference of the Western Association of State Game and Fish Commissioners, Vancouver, B.C. Mimeographed.

1959.   *Wildlife of Mexico.* Berkeley and Los Angeles: University of California Press.

1966.   "Adaptability of Animals to Habitat Change." In *Future Environments of North America*, edited by F. Fraser Darling and J. P. Milton, pp. 66–75. New York: Natural History Press.

1967.   "Grizzlies of the Sierra del Nido." *Pacific Discovery* 20, no. 5:30–32.

1969.   "Reports of the Special Advisory Board on Wildlife Management for the Secretary of the Interior, 1963–1968." Washington, D.C.: Wildlife Management Institute.

1974.   "Ecosystem Deterioration under Multiple Use." Wild Trout Management Symposium, Yellowstone National Park. Mimeographed.

1977a.   *The California Quail.* Berkeley and Los Angeles: University of California Press.

1977b.   "Meditations in a Duck Blind." *Gray's Sporting Journal*, Fall, pp. 6–10.

1978a.   "Wildlife and Forest Practice." In *Wildlife and America*, edited by H. Brokaw, pp. 108–120. Washington, D.C.: Council on Environmental Quality.

1978b.   "Wildlife in a Prodigal Society." *Transactions, Forty-third North American Wildlife Conference*, Washington, D.C., pp. 5–10.

1979.   "The Status of Wildlife and Wildlife Habitat on Fort Hunter Liggett, Monterey County." Mimeographed.

1981.   "The Future of Trout." *The Flyfisher* 14, no. 1:29–30.

ABOUT THE AUTHOR

A. Starker Leopold was Professor of Zoology and Forestry at the University of California, Berkeley. By the time of his death in 1983, he had become a leading figure in the study of the land and wildlife, receiving honors for his contributions to biological science, conservation, and education. Author of more than one hundred publications, Leopold did perhaps his most important work in the area of ornithology. Both *The California Quail* (1977) and *Wildlife of Mexico* (1959) received the Wildlife Publication Award for the best book of the year.

Deeply concerned about wildlife and resources management, Leopold played an influential role in many committees and organizations dedicated to conservation, including The Nature Conservancy, Sierra Club, Wilderness Society, National Wildlife Federation, and California Academy of Sciences. In 1962 he served as head of the advisory committee for the preservation of wilderness to Secretary of the Interior Stewart Udall.

ABOUT THE PHOTOGRAPHER

Tupper Ansel Blake is a naturalist and professional wildlife photographer. His photographs, known for their technical excellence and artistic quality, have been featured in numerous books and in such journals as *Audubon*, *National Geographic*, *National Wildlife*, *Smithsonian*, and *Sierra*. Exhibitions of his work have appeared at the United Nations and in museums all over the United States, including the Smithsonian Institution, the California Academy of Sciences, and the Dallas Museum of Natural History.

A skilled practitioner of the difficult art of photographing animals in their natural habitats, Blake was selected as the official still photographer for the U.S. Fish and Wildlife Service/National Audubon Society's California Condor Recovery Program and has also received the Sierra Club's 1985 Ansel Adams photography award. Currently he is conducting a photographic survey on "The Wetlands of Western North America/The Pacific Flyway" for the Smithsonian Institution.

Designer: Steve Renick
Compositor: G & S Typesetters, Inc.
Text: Mergenthaler Linotron 202 Bembo
Display: Bembo
Printer: Toppan Printing Co., Ltd.
Binder: Toppan Printing Co., Ltd.
Editorial Coordinator: Mary Renaud
Production Coordinator: Ellen Herman